SD-WAN The Networking Blueprint for Modern Businesses

Rohan Naggi, VeloCloud, now part of VMware
Rachna Srivastava, VeloCloud, now part of VMware

Foreword by **Steven Woo**, Co-founder and Sr. Director Product Management, VeloCloud, now part of VMware

The Next Wave of SD-WAN by **Sanjay Uppal**, Vice President and General Manager, VeloCloud Business Unit VMware

Driving innovation in Healthcare by **Frank Nydam**, VP Global Healthcare Alliances, VMware

Second Edition

 **vm**ware· PRESS

VMWARE PRESS

Program Manager
Rohan Naggi

Technical Writer
Jeff Baskin

Graphics Manager
Nathan Kawanishi, Jason Lee, Elinor Schott, Sappington

**SD-WAN The Networking Blueprint for Modern Businesses
Second Edition**
Printed in the United States of America
First Printing August 2018

Warning & Disclaimer

Every effort has been made to make this book as complete and as accurate as possible, but no warranty or fitness is implied. The information provided is on an "as is" basis. The authors, VMware Press, VMware, and the publisher shall have neither liability nor responsibility to any person or entity with respect to any loss or damages arising from the information contained in this book.

The opinions expressed in this book belong to the author and are not necessarily those of VMware.

Table of Contents

List of Figures

About the Authors

Rohan Naggi, Sr. Technical Product Manager at VeloCloud, now part of VMware focuses on service provider and large enterprise SD-WAN deployments. Rohan has been intimately involved in the WAN arena for over 10 years, having worked at Cisco Systems on WAN optimization and other solutions ranging from routing, security and SD-WAN. A sought-after public speaker, Rohan has presented at conferences and participated in panel discussions at a variety of global industry events. Rohan has a BE in Computer Technology.
Follow Rohan on Twitter: @lifeboy

Rachna Srivastava, Sr. Manager, Product Marketing at VeloCloud, now part of VMware is responsible for market research, enterprise content marketing, messaging framework, and planning and executing successful launch campaigns. She has long been involved in information technology with marketing and management positions at the industry's most innovative companies – developing and taking to market products that power some of the largest enterprises in the networking and datacenter industry.
Follow Rachna on Twitter: @Rachna_Sriv

Technical Reviewers

Tim Van Herck, Director Technical Product Management at VMware has over 15 years of experience in Technical Marketing, Product Management, and Cloud Service Operations. He is currently the Director of Technical Product Management at VeloCloud, now part of VMware, leading his team responsible for writing product content, technical training and development. Tim previously worked for Aryaka, Cisco Systems, Allegro Systems, Assured Access Technology and Alcatel. Tim holds an MS in Industrial Sciences from the University of Antwerp.

Madelyn Grunewald, Sr. Product Marketing Manager at VMware drives thought leadership and global go-to-market activities with technical partners for the NSX Portfolio and the Virtual Cloud Network vision. Madelyn worked for over 6 years in enterprise IT for financial services, holds an MBA from Chicago Booth and studied Mathematics-Computer Science at UCSD. Follow Madelyn on Twitter: @verdantblue

Technical Contributor
Chapter 3, Digital Transformation in Healthcare

Naman Sharma, Staff Systems Engineer in the Networking and Security Business Unit at VMware has deep expertise in WAN/data center networking and is committed to simplifying and revolutionizing digital business through Network Virtualization. He has served as a consulting architect and design engineer, helping customers implement and support next generation network architectures at scale, across a broad set of industries. Follow Naman on Twitter: @naman_31

Acknowledgments

First and most importantly, I would like to thank Almighty God for everything. I would like to thank my parents, and my sons Ayaan and Rehan for motivating and encouraging me. I would like to thank my lovely wife, Nargis, for supporting me – not only during the writing of this book, but with many endeavors throughout my technical career. None my achievements could have been possible without your support. I love you all.

Follow Rohan on Twitter: @lifeboy

Rohan Naggi
Sr. Technical Product Manager at VMware

Writing a book was a lot harder than I thought, and much more rewarding than I could have imagined. None of this would have been possible without the support of my family - my husband Rakesh, my sister Richa, and my two lovely kids Ronit and Meera. I also owe my deepest gratitude to my co-author and friend, Rohan for a solid partnership in this journey. SD-WAN is here to stay and is making a huge impact on the way organizations run and manage their networks. This book is a humble attempt to introduce our readers to SD-WAN and how VMware SD-WAN by VeloCloud™ can unify the edge, datacenter, and the cloud.

Follow Rachna on Twitter: @Rachna_Sriv

Rachna Srivastava
Sr. Manager, Product Marketing at VMware

Our Gratitude

We would like to thank the VMware and VeloCloud family for their guidance and support. A special mention to the founders of VeloCloud - *Sanjay Uppal, Steven Woo*, and *Ajit Mayya* for their vision and leadership.

We would like to extend a special recognition to *Tim Van Herck* and *Kangwarn Chinthammit*, who have been extremely supportive during this journey. A special thanks to *Ravi Sharma, Ratnesh Sharma, Rajeev Singh* and our *marketing team* for their support.

We owe our gratitude to *Madelyn Grunewald, Katie Holms* and *Shinie Shaw* for providing clarity and guidance during the book writing process.

For the Healthcare content, we would like to extend our thanks to *Naman Sharma*. We would also like to extend our thanks to VMware Healthcare Management team *Scott Martin, Bill Roche* and *Paul Byrne* for their support.

Special thanks to technical reviewers for Healthcare content *Scott Martin, Mike Lonze* and *Dwayne Sinclair* for taking out time reviewing this in such a short span of time.

Finally, we would like to thank our readers. We hope you find this book a helpful resource in your own efforts to power business growth and success through technology. If you have any comments or suggestions about this book, we welcome your feedback.

Preface

In this book, we will discuss some of the new challenges that enterprises face in keeping their branch office users connected and productive. We will explore some of the reasons why traditional wide area network (WAN) architectures cannot keep up with escalating application needs, increasing complexity, and the increased use of Software-as-a-Service (SaaS) and cloud services. We will discuss how SD-WAN lets enterprises bypass the limitations of WANs based entirely on leased lines, through a software-defined approach.

Next, we will provide an overview of VMware SD-WAN by VeloCloud™. We will discuss its key components and deployment models and show how it lets enterprises of any size support application growth, enhance agility, and simplify and accelerate branch deployments and management.

Finally, we'll present some examples of how VMware SD-WAN is delivering dramatic benefits across a wide range of industries, including retailers, hospitality, healthcare, construction, and Internet of Things (IoT) and manufacturing environments.

Goal of This Book

The goal of this book is to educate readers about SD-WAN technologies, and its advantages compared to traditional WAN architectures. The book will provide an overview of key features and capabilities enabled by VMware SD-WAN by VeloCloud and show how it can aid enterprises in modernizing their WAN networks for assured application delivery and lower operating costs.

Foreword

You've probably heard about how SD-WAN is transforming the way companies connect their remote locations with headquarters and each other, as well as expanding cloud locations. We hope this book shows you how our vision for using software-defined control and agility, combined with the ease of cloud services, can transform your network. SD-WAN lets you escape complex, expensive and static WAN architectures and move toward a more agile approach based on software, virtualization and the cloud. We are thrilled that SD-WAN has become the accepted approach for building your WAN.

What does this mean in the real world? What if you could set up a new branch at a remote construction site in less than an hour? Provide better healthcare outcomes by delivering high-resolution patient scans and quality voice and video communications to remote clinics, using inexpensive broadband links? Ensure critical applications for keeping far flung manufacturing sites running are always available across the variety of circuits and providers at diverse geographic regions? SD-WAN makes it possible. And VMware SD-WAN by VeloCloud has more advantages than any other solution.

In this book, we'll talk about some of the changes that are driving so many enterprises to adopt SD-WAN. We'll discuss how technologies like virtualization, cloud, and as-a-service models are shaking up the rules for keeping extended organizations connected. And we'll explore why traditional architectures and management tools have trouble keeping up with complexity, new business models, and changing expectations.

We will walk you through some of the basic concepts behind SD-WAN, and show how its software-defined approach can help any enterprise WAN become more agile, dependable, and open. And we will discuss some of the features that make VMware SD-WAN by VeloCloud the platform of choice for so many forward-looking customers.

To help spark ideas about how SD-WAN can benefit your organization, we've included several short examples that showcase its capabilities for many different industries. You'll see VMware SD-WAN at work in healthcare, retail, manufacturing, IoT, and more, and understand the business outcomes it delivers. We hope this book helps answer some of your questions about SD-WAN and inspires you to learn more about how it can transform your organization.

Steven Woo
Co-Founder and Vice President of Products
VeloCloud (now part of VMware)

Chapter 1

Introduction: Tomorrow's WAN Has Arrived

This first chapter presents core concepts of Software-Defined Wide Area Networks (SD-WANs). We will discuss how networking needs have evolved as businesses consume applications and services in new and different ways. We will also explore some of the key features and benefits of SD-WAN.

Challenges: Moving Beyond Yesterday's WAN

Most businesses have witnessed major technology changes over the past ten to fifteen years. Not so long ago, keeping a business connected and productive on a wide area network (WAN) was a relatively rigid but straightforward process. Most applications and workloads resided on-premises in data centers where IT could directly monitor and manage them. To access needed resources, branch sites simply connected to those resources via the WAN (Figure 1.1) User traffic was more predictable, flowing directly from each branch site to the data center and back again. Organizations connected everything together with technologies like Multiprotocol Label Switching (MPLS), leased lines, and other types of dedicated private links.

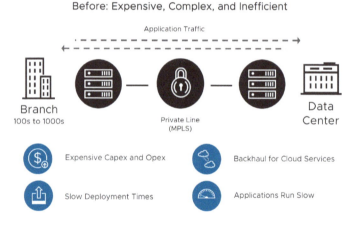

Before: Expensive, Complex, and Inefficient

Figure 1.1 Traditional Point-to-Point WAN

When it was time to add more bandwidth or expand to a new branch location, IT would have to purchase more leased lines and painstakingly set up and configure routers and switches at the new site.

Internet access for users was typically backhauled through the data center, where centralized firewalls offered security services for traffic destined for public sites. Centralizing the Internet breakout allowed organizations to use private circuits for Internet traffic, creating fewer egress points on the network and effectively reducing its external attack surface. However, this approach also resulted in extra latency, as applications needed to detour through a central point to reach their destination.

Today's Applications and Architectures Require a Fresh Approach

Today, the emergence of technologies like cloud, virtualization, and as-a-service models have upended the traditional rules for extended enterprise networking. In a multi-cloud world, many organizations are being forced to reconsider how they connect and unify their dispersed sites.

Management trends and practices are changing, and network teams are facing increasing pressure to unify and centralize control while providing the most optimal path to applications over their diverse environments. Enterprises are looking for better ways to reduce costs by minimizing local support and licensing expenses as well as reducing equipment footprint and deployment complexity. They also want to improve security and ensure that their most critical data is protected. Compliance has become more important, and organizations are looking for better ways to stay in line with changing government and industry regulations.

Network applications have also evolved. Today's WAN must support connectivity not only between traditional data applications, but also latency-sensitive real time applications like Voice over IP (VoIP) and videoconferencing. Organizations employ these bandwidth-intensive applications not only in the office environment, but in everything from communication and collaboration to digital signage, physical security, and surveillance.

Finally, the pace of business change is accelerating, making agility more important. The IT infrastructure is a key enabler and driver of innovation and business growth. Stakeholders expect network teams to offer rapid access to the technology resources they need and easily scale them up (or down) when business requirements change. In a fast-paced world of digital transformation, it is simply unacceptable for the network to be a bottleneck in delivering on-demand infrastructure. At the same time, there is an implicit expectation that the network is always available. Even a brief network outage can cause a significant disruption to the business.

Let us take a closer look at some of the top challenges that network teams face in this rapidly changing landscape. We will discuss how SD-WAN can help position organizations to address key IT concerns in the near term, and we will also look forward and explore how SD-WAN can serve as a foundation to modernize the enterprise for the future.

Last Mile Network Designs are the Weak Link in Cloud Computing

Organizations are rapidly adopting cloud and as-a-service solutions, as the shift to Software-as-a-Service (SaaS) gains momentum. We are seeing many more organizations moving their business-critical systems to solutions like Salesforce.com, Amazon Web Services (AWS), Google G Suite, and Microsoft Office 365. Leveraging best-of-breed services in the cloud allows the provider of such services to customize the hosting facility to the needs of the application. It also lets providers employ custom security solutions to protect against abuse and malicious use of the service. Organizations no longer need to plan and operate infrastructure to host software solutions when they are available as a SaaS offering.

A recent survey by Rightscale reported that overall Microsoft Azure adoption grew from 34 to 45 percent of respondents over the past year, while AWS adoption grew from 57 to 64 percent of respondents over the same period.[1]

Organizations of all sizes are convinced of the potential of cloud as a powerful, agile business enabler. However, their network teams are facing major challenges in addressing new demands. All too often the rigid architectures, cost, and complexity of their existing WAN are holding their organizations back – particularly in branch offices where changes happen frequently. Multi-cloud organizations take a performance hit when they backhaul Internet-bound traffic from the branches over the data center and then out to the public Internet. Although backhauling network traffic can deliver the level of service that enterprises require, it consumes excessive amounts of limited—and expensive—private bandwidth.

69% say demand for WAN bandwidth is expected to increase either significantly (20%) or somewhat (49%).[2]

Enterprises are grappling with increasingly complex networks that are difficult to manage. They are employing a variety of WAN circuits, although they face a common set of business challenges. Organizations need the ability to manage and control these multiple WAN circuits, even as bandwidth usage is increasing, and more traffic shifts toward cloud destinations (Figure 1.2). At the same time, they must steer application traffic across multiple circuits and links, using their existing WAN solutions.

Furthermore, a WAN will only be as effective as the last mile that interconnects the customer premises to the service provider core network. Since cable systems, telephone wires or fibers are commonly

1 "Cloud Computing Trends: 2018 State of the Cloud Survey," Rightscale
2 Interop ITX Research, August 2017

used to deliver this connection, they are also the most exposed to environmental factors such as changing moisture conditions or construction activity that can reduce or completely disrupt the quality of the signal carried.

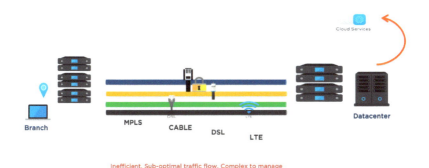

Inefficient, Sub-optimal traffic flow, Complex to manage

Figure 1.2 Challenges with Multiple Disparate Links and Cloud Migration

To overcome these issues, organizations need a flexible, secure, and dependable way to offer local Internet breakout access to cloud applications that drive their business. They need a solution that brings end-to-end visibility, management control, and secure connectivity from the branch to the cloud and data center.

Cloud technologies are based on flexibility, and organizations want to make the most of it. They require flexible and versatile deployment options for their cloud environment. At the same time, they want to avoid vendor lock-in that limits flexibility in the future. The solution must also provide resilience and a mechanism to steer traffic to the best-performing links, in case a network impairment event takes place that impacts the end-user experience. Network impairments such as packet loss, jitter and high latency can be caused by environmental changes as well because of peering congestion and can cause significant impact on application performance.

Management is Complex and Cumbersome

Managing WAN solutions for enterprise branch offices using traditional techniques is not easy in an environment that is rapidly evolving with applications increasingly moving to the cloud.

Technologies like Quality of Service (QoS) and the configuration of such solutions often require manual efforts that are cumbersome and prone to human error. IT professionals must manually enter parameters like bandwidth allocation and queuing mechanisms for each application on every device. When parameters change, manually reconfiguring the solution can introduce errors and involve expensive site visits. Configuration tasks are more complex, because application detection is no longer as simple as entering a TCP port.

Furthermore, QoS is based on the assumptions that an administrator knows how much bandwidth is available; that the bandwidth is constant; and that they know and understand which applications require a distinct slice of available bandwidth in the event congestion occurs. Although these assumptions are true for MPLS circuits, when working with broadband circuits bandwidth is highly variable. QoS is targeted to ensure that critical applications continue to operate as expected under congestion conditions, such as narrow band links. Making broadband links available to the enterprise can help mitigate congestion concerns, giving administrators the option to offer 10 to 100 times more bandwidth. However, adding broadband access can introduce new challenges around the quality of the bandwidth, since it is no longer governed by a service-level agreement (SLA) that guarantees network availability and packet delivery characteristics.

Traditional management tools have limitations as well. They cannot provide the centralized visibility and control that network teams need to consolidate management and ensure security and compliance. As infrastructures grow and evolve over time, most organizations accumulate a variety of different management tools for different functions. They may have different tools for security and QoS configurations, troubleshooting, branch on-boarding, and other capabilities. Each tool often requires individual expertise from different IT personnel. Even when these tools provide centralized management, they frequently require templates that must be completed for each of the provisioned sites. Working with templates is a tedious process that is prone to human error. Network administrators prefer to convey an intent for how sites should behave without having to work through the minute details for each site.

These disparate tools and skill sets make it difficult for network teams to monitor and address network reliability, bandwidth, and latency. If an issue arises, troubleshooting can be difficult and time-consuming—causing network reliability issues that can impact the bottom line. To minimize management complexity, network teams need a single tool that lets them configure, manage, monitor, analyze, and troubleshoot across their entire infrastructure.

Legacy Networks Are Not Built for Today's Edge Needs

Traditional WAN architectures also face challenges because they are not designed for today's edge-powered requirements. As organizations get more mobile and hyper-connected, there is an increasing amount of activity at the network edge from Internet of

Things (IoT) applications and devices, as well as mobile devices and communication clients. Supporting these edge applications, especially bandwidth-intensive applications like real-time voice, video, and data is challenging. The network edge requires more control and real-time decisions.

A recent survey estimated 248 million desktop video conferencing users globally and determined 79% of global Internet traffic will be video in 2020.[3]

Ensuring the delivery of time-sensitive applications introduces more network complexity. Organizations often find themselves in situations where the branch bandwidth is insufficient, or the aging infrastructure cannot support unified communications needs. Upgrading the WAN to support these requirements can be expensive and delay the rollout of other new services and applications.

Broadband connections are not reliable enough to support critical business applications, so most enterprises prefer to send their data over MPLS lines that offer more robust security. Furthermore, broadband connections cannot provide the application-level SLAs that MPLS can offer for performance-sensitive applications. Broadband Internet options can experience regional peering congestion which results in increased latency, packet loss, and jitter that degrades performance of real-time applications.

Network teams need a cost-effective solution that lets them extend high-quality communications from the edge to the data center, to the cloud, across an increasingly extended organization—using the connectivity option of their choice.

Manual Configuration Hampers Business Agility

Traditional WAN environments require device-by-device configuration, usually with direct, command-line interface processes. When it is time to set up new branch sites, each configuration must be customized and manually entered. Organizations might even employ separate network teams, tools, and processes to support different parts of their network, security, servers, and applications.

A software-defined, policy-based approach to new service deployment can change everything. With tools like automation and zero-touch configuration, network teams can rapidly deliver the connectivity and services that their business stakeholders demand. With the right level of agility, organizations can gain fast access to the resources they need to keep pace with disruptive competitors.

3 VNI Index, 2018

Application Programming Interface (API) and Software Development Kit (SDK) integration to existing management systems or new cloud-based management services can enable organizations to enhance their agility. It lets them shift their focus from finding an application that contains all the required features, to offering an ecosystem of applications where data can be securely exchanged as needed.

To deliver the technology their business stakeholders need to get to market faster and innovate better, network teams need to move beyond boxes toward a more agile infrastructure.

Solution: Enter SD-WAN

As networks have become more complex, organizations have turned to software-defined networking (SDN) to help improve the efficiency and manageability of their infrastructure. SDN is an architectural model for networking, and there are many ways to implement it. The key to SDN is that it abstracts the network to a set of capabilities that are independent of how those capabilities are provided. Therefore, an application using the network will not have to include specifics of the network equipment or other details that may change regularly.

SD-WAN takes the principles of SDN and applies them to the WAN, to deliver similar advantages. SD-WAN is considered one of the first practical SDN applications. Both SDN and SD-WAN segregate control and data planes to independently apply the scaling and redundancy mechanism best suited for the plane. Furthermore, virtualized resources provide accelerated services delivery, better performance, and improved availability by automating network deployment and management, while reducing the total cost of ownership.

SD-WAN provides a software abstraction layer to create a network overlay and decouple network software services from the underlying hardware WAN circuits (Figure 1.3). This new abstraction lets network administrators control and manage networks more easily than was possible using traditional approaches for managing underlying WAN hardware. SD-WAN is a network overlay that provides a common transport layer across different physical components and network links, to simplify the overall network administration and enable network owners to develop their own infrastructure-independent applications.

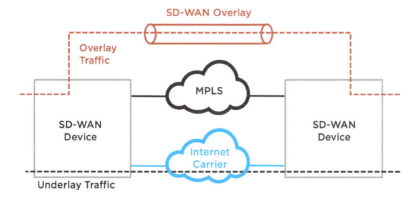

Figure 1.3 SD-WAN Overlay Tunnel on Multiple Links.

How SD-WAN Benefits Network Teams

SD-WAN empowers organizations to meet business-critical priorities at the edge by enabling rich deployment, management, and scaling capabilities. It enables network teams to cost-effectively provide the connectivity and performance that dispersed organizations need while maintaining deep control and visibility across the infrastructure. This unleashes several benefits, including:

Optimized cloud architecture: SD-WAN does away with the need for the backhaul of network traffic employed in MPLS and other traditional networks—and its associated performance problems. SD-WAN lets organizations utilize public links to provide secure, high-performance connections from the branch to cloud. This cloud architecture also lets organizations support local Internet breakout with firewalling.

A more agile, flexible business: SD-WAN makes it fast, easy and cost effective for organizations to deploy the WAN services they need to support branch operations, without requiring an IT professional working directly at the site. When needs change, it is easy to add more bandwidth through inexpensive broadband circuits or by quickly setting up WAN services such as bandwidth and firewalls at distributed branch sites.

Internet economics: SD-WAN delivers the power of choice, freeing organizations to select from a variety of Internet connectivity options. These options are fast and easy to install and set up. Best of all, it lets organizations take advantage of secure, dependable WAN services at a much more cost-effective price point compared to MPLS links, to augment network connectivity.

Adopt fast, manage easily: Speed and business agility are essential for every business. SD-WAN solutions are straightforward to deploy, and they utilize centralized provisioning to eliminate the need for trained personnel to visit remote sites.

Ability to leverage hybrid WAN: Most distributed organizations already have MPLS connecting their branch offices. SD-WAN lets them easily complement MPLS with one or more broadband links without modifying the existing MPLS network. When requirements change, organizations can continue to migrate traffic growth toward cost-effective Internet bandwidth, freeing up MPLS links to serve applications that have specific performance or compliance requirements.

Automation and traffic steering: SD-WAN gives organizations the ability to prioritize traffic. It offers tools for setting priorities, as well as the ability to automatically change traffic flows to stay in sync with dynamic network conditions.

What You Need to Know

- Evolving technology has transformed the way branch offices connect via the WAN, and current architectures cannot keep pace with today's advanced applications and multi-cloud environments.

- Traditional techniques for managing enterprise WANs are complex, manual, and error-prone.

- SD-WAN takes the principles of SDN and applies them to the WAN, to deliver similar advantages in agility and manageability.

- SD-WAN lets organizations utilize public links to provide secure, high-performance connections from the branch to cloud, for rich deployment options, improved management, and superior scaling capabilities.

Chapter 2

VMware SD-WAN by VeloCloud: A Smarter Approach to SD-WAN

Now that we have explored SD-WAN essentials, let us take a closer look at how VMware SD-WAN by VeloCloud™ delivers on these capabilities. We will focus on its key components, core capabilities, and the unique features that set VMware SD-WAN apart from other offerings.

The Foundation of the Virtual Cloud Network

VMware SD-WAN by VeloCloud is part of the VMware NSX family, with products such as NSX Data Center, NSX Cloud, AppDefense, vRealize Network Insight, and NSX Hybrid Connect. Together, these products form the foundation of the Virtual Cloud Network, delivering secure and pervasive connectivity for applications and data—from the data center to the cloud and to the edge.

VMware SD-WAN can work with or without the NSX product family.

Its broad range of capabilities are ideal for both enterprises and service providers.

Gartner[4] specifies four key capabilities as critical for SD-WAN. VMware SD-WAN delivers and meets all of these essential requirements and takes them a step further (Figure 2.1). It provides:

- Lightweight replacement for traditional WAN routers and support for multiple connection types

- Dynamic path selection for load sharing and policy-based operation

- A simple, intuitive WAN management and monitoring interface

- Support for secure VPNs and integrated third-party network services

VMware SD-WAN complements Gartner's key capabilities by offering:

- Deep Application Recognition (DAR) engine, capable to identifying over 3,000 applications through well-known address ranges and ports, as well as flow heuristics

- A hosted service offering creating an instant global footprint, providing optimized access to most commonly-used SaaS applications

- An open ReST API and complementary SDKs provide rapid development for integration into existing OSS/BSS systems as well as other operational software components that benefit from the information collected by the VMware SD-WAN Orchestrator, which we will discuss below.

4 https://www.telecomramblings.com/2017/09/focus-makes-difference-sd-wan-vendors

Transport Independent   **Secure Overlay**   **Dynamic Path Selection**   **Simple Interface**

VMware SD-WAN by VeloCloud
Complements with Additional Capabilities

• Broadband	• Cloud VPN	• DMPO	• Zero Touch Provisioning
• LTE	• Application Firewall	• Deep Application Recognition	• Orchestrator
• MPLS (Hybrid)		• Live Link Measurement	• ReST API

Figure 2.1 Key Capabilities of SD-WAN Solution as defined by Gartner and VMware SD-WAN Capabilities

VMware SD-WAN enables enterprises to securely support application growth, network agility, and simplified branch implementations. It also provides support for delivery of high-performance, reliable branch access to cloud services, private data centers, and SaaS-based enterprise applications.

Suitable for distributed organizations of any size and industry segment, VMware SD-WAN is easy to deploy and can be provisioned through a cloud-based configuration and monitoring portal. With a range of flexible deployment options from on-premises, hybrid cloud and on-premises, and a complete cloud-based deployment, VMware SD-WAN can meet any organization's needs. It is delivered through a combination of distributed gateways located in the cloud, which are connected to edge devices located in each branch office.

VMware SD-WAN offers the unique ability for enterprises to keep their existing WAN while implementing a transition to SD-WAN. It interoperates smoothly with existing infrastructures, while enabling organizations to add capacity or strengthen reliability via links such as additional Internet, cellular, MPLS, or other options. It can incorporate any WAN transport, whether private, public, or even wireless broadband links such as LTE. As more transport mechanisms standardize on Ethernet handoffs at the customer premises, any such link can be incorporated in the VMware SD-WAN bandwidth mix.

With VMware SD-WAN, organizations can accelerate their cloud application adoption with flexible traffic policies and provide support for their branch sites at a fraction of the cost of a traditional MPLS network.

VMware SD-WAN also enables local service providers to deliver advanced services and increase flexibility. With VMware SD-WAN, service providers can deliver elastic transport, performance for cloud applications, and integrate advanced services with a flexible deployment model.

Core VMware SD-WAN Capabilities

As a network overlay, VMware SD-WAN enables organizations to virtualize the network, so application traffic can be carried independently of the underlying physical or transport layer.

Three core capabilities power VMware SD-WAN: centralized management and flexibility; assured application performance; and the ability to act as a managed on-ramp to the cloud (Figure 2.2).

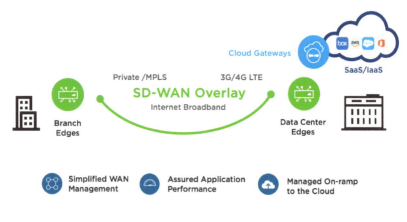

Figure 2.2 Key Differentiators for VMware SD-WAN

Centralized Management and Flexibility

As network infrastructures become increasingly distributed and complex, network teams need detailed visibility into off-net remote location network links, devices, and applications. They require immediate insight in real time, as well as the ability to view historical data to make informed decisions about the strategic direction of the network.

VMware SD-WAN's centralized monitoring, visibility, and cloud control enable zero-touch branch deployment across distributed locations while delivering automated business policy and firmware updates, link performance, and capacity measurements. VMware SD-WAN also supports northbound ReST APIs for integration with a variety of management solutions and multi-tenant dashboards for service providers. It supports automatic application recognition and categorization, to minimize routine networking tasks such as defining applications by their TCP/UDP ports and destination IP addresses.

With VMware SD-WAN, policies can be set and deployed with a click of the mouse button. Enterprises can set up business-level policies that apply enterprise wide across multiple edge sites, using a single, cloud-based orchestrator.

Assured Application Performance

VMware SD-WAN enables enterprises and service providers to utilize multiple WAN transports simultaneously under varying conditions while ensuring application performance. It employs unique Dynamic Multi-Path Optimization to boost the capacity and service capabilities of Internet as well as hybrid links. WAN circuits are continuously monitored for link and path quality, as well as available capacity. Applications are automatically recognized and steered to the optimal links based on business priority, built-in knowledge of application network requirements, real-time link performance, and capacity metrics. Dynamic per-packet steering can move a session—for example, a voice call—mid-stream to avoid link degradation without dropping the call or introducing voice quality issues. Single high bandwidth flows can utilize aggregated bandwidth for faster response times.

VMware SD-WAN applies remediation, including error correction, jitter buffering and local re-transmits, on-demand when only a single link is available or concurrent link degradations cannot be steered around. On-demand remediation is applied for priority applications that are network sensitive and when brownout link degradations occur.

VMware SD-WAN employs profiles that define how a site should process traffic according to business policies. For example, network teams may prefer to deploy a business-critical video conferencing application on an MPLS link, regardless of where the link is connected on the edge. VMware SD-WAN determines the MPLS link's port and applies QoS policies based on available bandwidth to prioritize the application.

The unique cloud-delivered architecture offers these benefits for on-premises and cloud applications (SaaS/IaaS).

Managed On-Ramp to the Cloud

VMware SD-WAN provides direct, secure, optimized access to cloud-based services, for organizations with a cloud strategy.

With VMware SD-WAN, enterprises can confidently connect to cloud services they require. Its transport-independent overlay delivers network performance, reliability, and manageability, at scale. Organizations can build a single tunnel to an IaaS provider, which can be accessed by all its edge sites. New edges immediately have access to all connected private cloud services. It is no longer necessary to connect every branch to all applications. Instead, an organization can simply connect its branches and applications to a fabric.

VMware SD-WAN helps organizations accelerate their cloud application adoption with flexible traffic policies, and support their branch sites by enabling local Internet breakouts and avoiding complex traffic backhaul through MPLS networks.

A Complete Solution Based on Three Key Components

VMware SD-WAN offers the key elements needed to achieve a cloud-delivered SD-WAN: a cloud network for enterprise-grade connection to cloud and enterprise applications; software-defined control and automation; and virtual services delivery.

VMware SD-WAN is unique in its ability to support data plane services in the cloud, in addition to on-premise deployments; enabling policy-based access to cloud and data center applications. It leverages the economics of the cloud so organizations can ease adoption and scale easily. Furthermore, it can be easily integrated into service provider networks and offer value-added services directly attached to the private core network.

VMware SD-WAN consists of three components: the VMware SD-WAN Edge, VMware SD-WAN Gateways, and the VMware SD-WAN Orchestrator.

VMware SD-WAN Edge

The VMware SD-WAN Edge is an enterprise-class appliance (physical or virtual) that provide secure, optimized connectivity to private, public and hybrid applications, compute and virtualized services, and is the component that is most visible to the organization. It can recognize over 3,000 applications and performs application and packet steering, on-demand remediation, performance metrics, and end-to-end QoS.

The VMware SD-WAN Edge can run as a Virtual Network Function (VNF) in Universal Customer Premise Equipment (uCPE), delivering exceptional deployment flexibility. The VMware SD-WAN Edge also supports a platform to host multiple VNFs, enabling network teams to eliminate single-function appliances and reduce branch IT complexity.

VMware SD-WAN Orchestrator

The VMware SD-WAN Orchestrator, residing on premises or in the cloud, provides centralized enterprise-wide installation, configuration and real-time monitoring in addition to orchestrating the data flow through the network. This component enables one-click provisioning of virtual services in the branch, the cloud, or the enterprise data center. It also provides end-to-end visibility from the LAN to the data center.

The VMware SD-WAN Orchestrator employs configuration profiles to manage the solution. These profiles encourage uniform policy distribution and simplify business policy rules by identifying applications that are critical to the business. Profiles let network administrators define the intent for how site should behave, and process application traffic in the larger enterprise context. They enable administrators to sidestep tedious configuration of every site. Instead, network teams can adjust policies based on local (edge) networking conditions and the business intent specified in the profile.

When service providers deploy the solution on-premises, they can benefit from a multi-tenancy approach found in all the infrastructure components.

VMware SD-WAN Gateway

VMware SD-WAN Gateways are the third major component of the solution, providing an optimized cloud on-ramp to the doorstep of SaaS and IaaS offerings. VMware SD-WAN incorporates a distributed network of service gateways deployed at top tier cloud data centers around the world, providing scalability, redundancy and on-demand flexibility.

They are fully automated, and managed and operated by VMware SD-WAN, but also offer flexible consumption options and can run in partner or service provider networks. They can also be used to extend SD-WAN connectivity from branches to legacy data centers.

Organizations can use VMware SD-WAN Edge devices to connect to a system of global VMware SD-WAN Gateways to provide performance, security and visibility for cloud services (SaaS, IaaS, B2B Internet). VMware SD-WAN Gateways are an ideal option for customers who want secure, reliable connectivity to the internet directly from their branches. Data centers that do not utilize VMware SD-WAN Edge devices can connect branches to VMware SD-WAN Gateways, with a direct IPSec link from the VMware SD-WAN Gateway to the data center.

For service providers, VMware SD-WAN Gateways provide multi-tenancy support, strictly segregating traffic between tenants when it is received from VMware SD-WAN Edge devices and forwarded to its final destination.

An Architecture That Protects Investments

Organizations of all sizes as well as Service Providers can benefit from the advantages VMware SD-WAN services bring to the table. In both cases, it allows the consumer of the service to deploy hybrid networks that include public (Internet) and private (e.g. MPLS) links and reduce the risk of an impairment on one link impacting the end-user experience at the branch site.

Enterprise Over-The-Top Deployment

Organizations have made substantial investments in their network infrastructures as well as have long term contracts for bandwidth in place. Performing infrastructure forklift upgrades is cost-prohibitive as well as disruptive. Today's organizations are seeking to make better use of their existing networking assets without major modifications to their infrastructure, while providing a pathway to reduce complexity in each branch location. VMware SD-WAN is the solution of choice to accommodate these initiatives.

In an over-the-top architecture (OTT), edges are installed at the customer premises, while consume control and data plane services reside in the cloud (Figure 2.3). The management plane is provided by the VMware SD-WAN Orchestrator, and a distributed control and optional data plane manifests itself through a series of horizontally scalable gateways. Edges can build overlays over both public and private circuits to provide access to applications and resources hosted in a corporate data center—whether physical, or a virtual data center implemented at an IaaS provider.

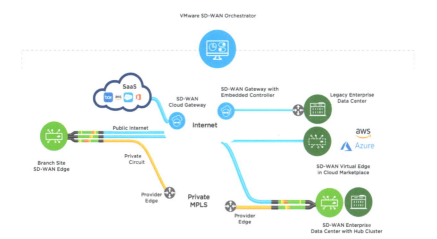

Figure 2.3 Enterprise Over the Top Deployment of VMware SD-WAN

SD-WAN Integrated with Service Providers

VMware SD-WAN components can also be integrated into existing service provider network architectures (Figure 2.4). The solution offers a three tier, multi-tenant, role-based orchestration portal for service providers to manage customers as well as partners. VMware SD-WAN Gateways are also multi-tenant capable, enabling efficient resource utilization and component re-use on the underlying hardware, while promoting portability. This allows data, management, and control plane components to be provisioned ahead of time and be ready to onboard customers at a moment's notice.

Unlike OTT deployments, the VMware SD-WAN Orchestrator and Gateways are deployed inside the service provider network offering the SD-WAN service. Gateways are installed at the nexus of public and private networks to allow VMware SD-WAN Edges to build overlays over both public and private links. This deployment model terminates the overlay at the service provider edge network, allowing unfettered access to the MPLS core network for long distance transport. They also provide access to hosted services attached to the customer context of the core network. For example, service providers can offer private Call Management Services (IP PBX) directly attached to the MPLS customer context, to reduce the complexity of the branch network. This is possible because the overlay network increases reliability of these centralized services.

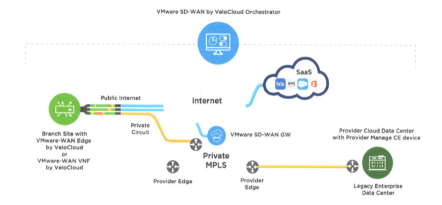

Figure 2.4 SD-WAN Integrates Seamlessly with Service Providers

Enabled by a Uniquely Powerful Feature Set

VMware SD-WAN lets enterprises build on their existing investments in WAN infrastructures, while taking advantage of the benefits of a software-defined architecture. Its rich feature set includes:

- **Analytics and visibility:** VMware SD-WAN by VeloCloud provides deep insight into which applications are being used, whether all links are being fully utilized, and how much of the network is being utilized by unsanctioned applications. It provides true path visibility that enables network teams to understand traffic flows end-to-end across the WAN. Intelligent analytics enable VMware SD-WAN by VeloCloud to continuously compute a quality score that reflects the performance of critical voice, video, or data applications at any given time. If an issue arises, it can automatically alert IT staff for remediation. This analysis gives administrators a full view into application behavior on individual links, as well as enhancements enabled by VMware SD-WAN.

- **Cloud VPN:** VMware SD-WAN by VeloCloud enables one-click, site-to-site cloud VPN, enabling organizations to connect VMware SD-WAN and non-VMware SD-WAN enabled sites—while offering real-time monitoring of their health. This Virtual Private Network Consortium (VPNC)-compliant IPSec VPN lets organizations set up secure dynamic edge-to-edge communication for all types of branches based on service level objectives and application performance. New branches can join the VPN network automatically, with access to all resources available at other branches, enterprise data centers, and third-party data centers. Organizations can choose from three options, employing logical technologies that differ by segment. These options include:

- ○ Hub-and-spoke topology

- ○ Branch-to-branch using a gateway or hub

- ○ Dynamic branch-to-branch

The branch-to-branch deployment using a gateway approach offers distinct advantages, enabling organizations to scale VPN connections without hair-pinning branch traffic all the way to the data center. With this approach, data center bandwidth is not utilized for branch-to-branch communication.

- **Security:** To help protect sensitive data and assets, VMware SD-WAN features a stateful, context-aware (application, user, device) integrated next-generation firewall. This firewall service enables granular control of micro-applications, along with support for applications with a dynamic and unpredictable flow nature, such as Skype. The firewall also makes it easy for organizations to segregate voice, video, data, and compliance traffic. Organizations can list and manage all their applications by category, applying broad policies for specific types of applications, with overrides for applications that must be treated differently. They can also apply policies for bring your own device (BYOD) devices such as tablets and smart phones for use on the corporate network. For organizations with specialized requirements, VMware SD-WAN also supports cloud access security brokers (CASBs) and works seamlessly with security solutions from best-of-breed security partners.

- **End-to-end segmentation:** Enterprise segmentation lets organizations logically isolate data by line of business or another organizational structures. VMware SD-WAN supports segmentation using a virtual routing and forwarding (VRF)-like concept with simplified, per-segment topology insertion. Segmentation capabilities enable each segment to have its own VPN topology, business policy, and firewall rules. Segmentation also lets organizations apply distinct application policies to each segment for prioritization and control, on a per application basis. Organizations can easily deploy a segment to a branch, and not all branches need to carry all segments.

- **Cross-cloud monitoring and provisioning with APIs:** Provisioning new cloud services is easy with one-click virtual services insertion capability. It lets organizations employ business-defined policies to reduce costs and enjoy superior performance. To order new services, a user can simply login to a web-based cloud portal, choose the offering they want, and have it automatically configured and delivered via SD-WAN—without any additional intervention by the network team. ReST-based APIs enable organizations to integrate, monitor, and control cloud services via a single pane of glass, while SDKs are available for rapid application development. Organizations can automate business policy, software, and firmware updates and upgrades, link performance, and capacity measurements.

- **Deployment flexibility and reliability:** VMware SD-WAN offers flexible deployment options, including a hardware device with ability to run additional services as a VNF or a virtual form factor, allowing organizations dramatically reduce the branch office footprint. It supports seamless insertion and chaining of virtualized services—both on-premises and in the cloud.

The VMware SD-WAN Advantage

VMware SD-WAN provides the key components needed to achieve a cloud-delivered SD-WAN: a cloud network for enterprise-grade connection to cloud and enterprise applications; software-defined control and automation; and virtual services delivery.

VMware SD-WAN is unique in its ability to support data plane services in the cloud in addition to on-premises deployments – enabling policy-based access to cloud and data center applications. It leverages the economics of the cloud to offer a SaaS-like subscription price model so organizations can ease adoption and pay-as-they-grow.

The solution lets organizations unleash:

- **Performance and reliability:** Organizations can enable a dependable hybrid WAN with high performance over a variety of transport options. It supports a range of service providers to enable network teams to ensure the best possible performance even for demanding, latency-sensitive applications like voice and video.

- **Cloud network:** Enterprises can sidestep data center backhaul penalties with a cloud-ready network that delivers an optimal and secure path to public and private clouds. Its unique architecture employs cloud gateways to enable organizations to extend to any cloud data center or point of presence (POP).

- **Automation and orchestration:** Organizations can gain insight and control over their extended environments through centralized monitoring, visibility and cloud control, and zero-touch branch deployment. The solution lets them deliver a smart, out-of-the-box business policy framework. It also enables organizations to automate business policy, software, and firmware updates and upgrades, link performance, and capacity measurements.

- **Streamlined provisioning via APIs:** One the advantages of VMware SD-WAN by VeloCloud orchestration in the cloud is its ability to enable self-service provisioning. To order new services, a user can simply login to a Web portal, choose the offering they want, and have it automatically configured and delivered via SD-WAN—without any additional intervention by the network team. Open, interoperable SD-WAN tools and protocols such as ReST Application Programming Interfaces (APIs) are key to enabling rapid service setup.

Freeing Up IT for Better Things

VMware understands that the roles of network teams are evolving. Managing a network is no longer limited to keeping business processes up and running. It's about finding new and creative ways to use technology to deliver engaging experiences for customers.

VMware SD-WAN lets organizations take the worry out of delivering dependable, assured connectivity across their branch sites. Instead of focusing on manual, time-consuming management tasks, network teams can spend more of their time on innovation and business growth. VMware SD-WAN offers a powerful, scalable foundation to take organizations into a new era of digital transformation.

Before and After: The SD-WAN Difference

Before SD-WAN, traditional routers were used to terminating public and private links (Figure 2.5). Links were in active/standby mode with private links carrying business critical traffic. For security reasons, branch site to datacenter site, IPSec was configured on Internet links. If an active link failed, such as MPLS, traffic was interrupted, steered to Internet link, and sent over an IPSec tunnel. Internet/SaaS traffic was backhauled over private links to the datacenter firewall for inspection. Element Management (EMS) was done from the datacenter site and each network device might have its own management portal.

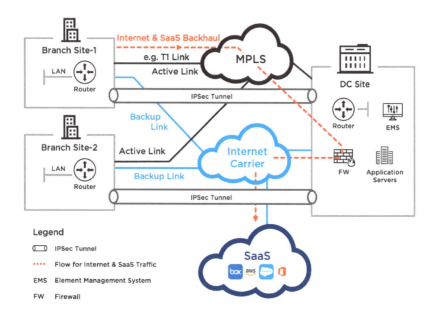

Figure 2.5 Network Blueprint Before SD-WAN

With VMware SD-WAN, routers are replaced with VMware SD-WAN Edges at the branch and data center sites (Figure 2.6). All links are in active/active mode, and any link can support overlay. Internet links now change their role from backup links to active links. This approach lets organizations employ MPLS links to transport only traffic that must meet compliance requirements, if they desire.

VMware SD-WAN eliminates backhaul of Internet/SaaS based application traffic to the datacenter which greatly decreases the risk of latency. Firewall roles can be pushed to branch sites with edge devices having integrated firewall services or utilizing a security VNF. EMS is replaced with a VMware SD-WAN Orchestrator that offers centralized command and control for configuring, monitoring, and troubleshooting the entire SD-WAN network.

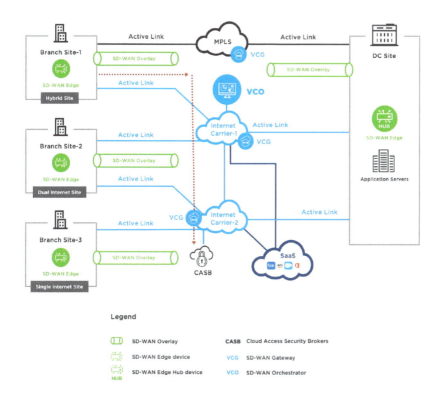

Figure 2.6 Network Blueprint with VMware SD-WAN

A variety of advanced inspection options are available for Internet/SaaS traffic (Figure 2.7), including:

1) Internet/SaaS traffic backhaul to datacenter with next-generation firewall

2) Branch to VMware SD-WAN Gateway

3) Direct branch breakout use case

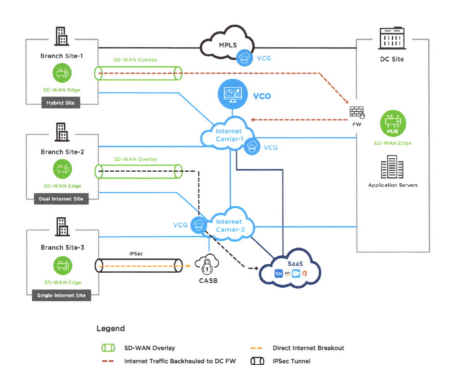

Legend

▭ SD-WAN Overlay		− − Direct Internet Breakout	
− − Internet Traffic Backhauled to DC FW		▭ IPSec Tunnel	
− − Internet and SaaS traffic from SD-WAN Gateway		FW Firewall	

Figure 2.7 Advanced Inspection Options for Internet/SaaS traffic with VMware SD-WAN

The Next Wave of SD-WAN

By Sanjay Uppal, Vice President and General Manager, VeloCloud Business Unit, VMware

IT is undergoing a sea change and is increasingly expanding to include Operations Technology (OT). Running a network is no longer limited solely to keeping business processes up and running. It's about finding new and creative ways to use technology to deliver engaging experiences for customers and about making an impact on the business.

As VMware SD-WAN continues to enable digital transformation, our customers expect more from their SD-WAN solution. With a 360° approach to innovation, we are solving customers' pain points, by being at the heart of their network from the branch and edge to the datacenter and cloud.

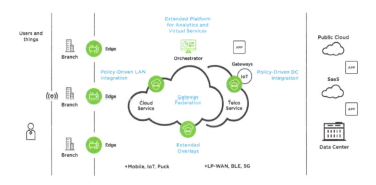

Figure 2.8 VMware SD-WAN 360° vision

VMware SD-WAN is expanding in scope to encompass connectivity from users and things to individual workloads in the data center. As the "east-west" scope expands, VMware SD-WAN by VeloCloud is evolving into a platform for additional network services, while running on an increasing set of underlay (transport) links and a broadening list of hardware devices from IOT gateways to purpose-built edge uCPE.

VMware SD-WAN by VeloCloud Expands to Users and Things

At the branch end, the SD-WAN Edge today sits at the termination point of the underlay (transport) links. The first step to associate the WAN traffic with Wi-Fi/LAN is to map the flow to LAN IP addresses and then to individual users. Performing this mapping automatically allows VMware SD-WAN to segment traffic from individual users through the WAN for performance and security reasons. The next step is to extend the end client from a user to a "thing". That thing can be a sensor, IoT Gateway, actuator, or any network addressable entity in the branch. Since there can be 10 to 100 times the number of things in the branch compared to users, there can be a real benefit to attracting IoT traffic onto the same enterprise SD-WAN as user traffic.

A critical development is in the offing where compute is moving back into the branch/edge primarily for reasons of providing a low latency result to a local query. Face recognition, mechanical response, and retail tracking are all examples of such applications. When compute moves back to the branch there is a tremendous benefit to look at the architecture in terms of a micro-datacenter and apply the same principles of large scale data centers to the branch—without any human intervention. VMware SD-WAN is paving the way to combine edge compute and IoT telemetry and response, with SD-WAN performance and security all under a single business policy.

VMware SD-WAN Expands into the Datacenter

Penetrating deeper into the datacenter and getting closer to workloads enables consistent policy management and end-to-end visibility from the datacenter to the branch. An individual WAN segment is mapped into an individual routing domain in the data center. This allows a single context in the branch to be directly connected to an individual workload in the data center. This extends the micro-segmentation concept for traffic within the data center to the context in the branch. The use cases for such branch to workload mapping abound in the retail and financial services spaces.

Extensible Platform for Analytics: Total Network Visibility and Application Control

Each VMware SD-WAN Edge acts as a sensor on the network collecting real-time information on both applications and the network, including usage and identity on the application side with network usage and performance on the WAN. Since the traffic originates at the end client and traverses the edge and the hub or gateway before going on to its destination, VMware SD-WAN has an unparalleled ability to provide telemetry on each flow and associate the flow to a user, IP address, and machine from the edge to the end application. The analytics are collected on a real-time basis across each enterprise and across all connected enterprises. The resultant data lets organizations detect issues, perform capacity planning and isolate problems with application performance down to the root cause.

VMware SD-WAN acts as a platform as the analytics are also fed into security information and event management (SIEM) and real-time dashboards. It enables network wide views of application behavior, underlay and overlay performance, and anomalies across the WAN, providing alerts and enabling technical teams to take action.The action involves human intervention today, but that is rapidly moving to an automated response as this rich set of data with billions of records is used to train AI systems for networking.

Extensible Overlay to Include Smart Phone and LP-WAN

With the advent of IoT, the choices for the underlay are increasing rapidly, both on the LAN and the WAN. Cellular connections using Cat-M and NB-IOT have been introduced by the carriers, while offerings such as Long range, low power wireless platform (LoRa) and others are examples of Low-power WAN (LPWAN) from the non-telco industry. Add LAN connections types like BLE, Zigbee and the like and the VMware SD-WAN Edge becomes an even broader overlay. Enterprise IoT traffic is particularly suited to the VMware SD-WAN architecture. A common business policy mechanism is used, and IoT data is simply another data type on the same SD-WAN providing consistency and efficiency across the business.

The number of hardware devices that SD-WAN runs on at the edge is also expanding rapidly. From low-end IoT gateways to larger micro or mini datacenters on the edge, the VMware SD-WAN Edge software in native or VNF form provides the application steering and control on the network. In the long-term we see the SD-WAN edge also penetrating end client devices including smart phones, smart TV's, and other devices.

Cloud Service and Telco Service Federation

VMware SD-WAN is provided as a cloud service, a telco service, or on-premises. The cloud service runs on gateways at IaaS and colo points of presence. The telco service runs on gateways at the telco POPS.

The gateway architecture enables per-packet or per-flow application steering and is also the point where additional services are inserted. When a telco wants to expand service into a region where they have not deployed gateways, such as off-net locations, they can federate their gateways with VMware SD-WAN deployed gateways. Gateway federation is a powerful mechanism to extend the overlay beyond on-net locations without gateway deployment. All the benefits of visibility and control accrue across the heterogenous network of gateways fulfilling the need to develop a global network with physical presence. The result? A true Software-Defined WAN.

What You Need to Know

- VMware SD-WAN provides the key elements needed to achieve a cloud-delivered SD-WAN: a cloud network for enterprise-grade connection to cloud and enterprise applications; software-defined control and automation; and virtual services delivery.

- Suitable for organizations in any industry, VMware SD-WAN is easy to deploy, and can be provisioned through a cloud-based configuration and monitoring portal.

- VMware SD-WAN consists of three key components, including the VMware SD-WAN Edge, VMware SD-WAN Orchestrator, and VMware SD-WAN Gateway.

- VMware SD-WAN employs an overlay technology that can be deployed as an over-the-top enterprise solution, without requiring organizations to "rip and replace" their existing networks.

Now It's Time to Put VMware SD-WAN by VeloCloud to Work...

We've discussed some of the challenges that extended organizations face today and explored how VMware SD-WAN can address them.

In the chapters that follow, we will take a closer look at how VMware SD-WAN can help organizations in a variety of industries solve the distinct challenges they face every day.

VMware SD-WAN can unlock benefits for enterprises of all sizes, including:

• Healthcare

• Retail

• Hospitality

• Construction

• IoT and the Industrial Internet of Things (IIoT)

• Enterprise

Chapter 3

Digital Transformation in Healthcare

Driving Innovation in Healthcare

By Frank Nydam
VP Global Healthcare Alliances

It has been 20 years since VMware literally redefined computing and helped usher in the era of the cloud. Ask anyone who discovered VMware early in their careers, and you will no doubt hear many fun stories about their first time seeing a virtual machine boot. They will likely describe it as jaw-dropping, unbelievable, magical and then will excitedly rattle off all the ways they started leveraging this amazing technology.

I was fortunate enough to join VMware in 2002. Since then I have had the opportunity to build healthcare solutions with some of the most talented and passionate technologists and industry professionals I have ever meet. Together with our partners, we help bring the power of our technology and people to bear on helping transform patient care.

Putting politics and policy aside, the last ten years of US Healthcare IT have been quite remarkable and dare I say historic. Healthcare was one of the last industries to digitize its business processes, and the impact of this historic transformation continues to ripple through the very fabric of our lives, economies, and the technology ecosystem.

During this time VMware has had the unique opportunity to help an entire industry safely accelerate its digital journey, and we also helped IT organizations become much more agile and efficient along the way. We pioneered the concept of 'follow-me' virtual desktops that enable caregivers to quickly and securely access patient data and images on practically any device. We are privileged to have helped the industry take its first and essential step towards its digital transformation journey.

Looking forward it is crucial that as an industry we do not lose sight of the original goals of this historic transformation; positively impacting the cost, quality, and delivery of patient care. We also need to focus an additional 'aim' and as an industry ensure that we do not overlook the care team experience and its impact on patient care.

We need to continue to empower caregivers with technology not "get in their way", by connecting patients directly to their data and caregiver from their mobile devices. Connecting, extracting and protecting valuable data from billions of connected things (IoT) that will help keep us safe and healthy. Digital transformation is enabling secure hyper-connected data sharing between and across organizations, with researchers and insurance providers. Seamlessly connecting public and private clouds and ushering in the multi-cloud era.

The authors of this book are technology trailblazers who have been bitten by the Healthcare 'bug'. They have discovered how even more powerful and fun technology can be when it can directly impact people's lives and well-being. This book will demonstrate how VMware's Software-Defined Networking and Security technology will once again help safely accelerate Healthcare's digital transformation.

I am genuinely optimistic and excited about the next ten years and what lies ahead.

"Tech as a force for good is not just our opportunity. It's our obligation." - Pat Gelsinger, CEO VMware

Frank Nydam
VP Global Healthcare Alliances

Frank Nydam is the Vice President of Global Healthcare Alliances and prior to that was Chief Technology Officer for Healthcare and Strategy at VMware. Frank joined VMware in 2002 and has been solely focused on the application of virtualization technologies in the Life Sciences and Healthcare Provider industry. He founded VMware's Healthcare program in 2007.

In his role, Frank collaborates with and across a broad range of Healthcare ecosystem partners including hospitals, application developers, and industry groups to help develop safer more efficient Healthcare solutions.

Before joining VMware, Frank was the Director of Technology at a national Microsoft Business Solutions partner responsible for application development and infrastructure services.

Frank holds a B.S. in Aerospace Mgt. from Kent State University, executive certificate(s) from Stanford University Graduate School for Design Thinking and Customer Focused Innovation as well as executive MBA's in Finance from Rutgers.Frank served a Board member of CHIME (College of Healthcare Information Management Executives) from 2015 – 2018.

Digital Transformation in Healthcare

In this chapter, we will explore how the Healthcare industry is providing a richer patient experience and how VMware SD-WAN by VeloCloud empowers healthcare providers & payers in delivering that regardless of location, while improving information technology (IT) productivity and efficiency.

In Healthcare, Technological advancements are paving way for more complex business requirements resulting in a rapid evolution of the industry. Technology has seen dramatic improvements in all aspects of patient care, from diagnostic imaging, scanning tools to the greater adoption of Electronic Medical Record (EMR) systems. Businesses are under pressure to deliver improved patient care in a consumer driven world. The Industry is consolidating with absorption of local clinics and rural practices into metropolitan and regional medical providers, and with large retailers acquiring pharmacies, minute clinics, and urgent care facilities. Network transformation is a critical factor in enabling success in today's business climate.

Consumerization of Healthcare is another important factor for the Healthcare industry. Patients are looking for simpler more streamlined access to all aspects of their care from interacting with their care teams to simplified and more transparent billing and payment systems. The result of this is an explosion in the number of access points and devices connected within Healthcare IT. Connectivity in healthcare now goes beyond the walls of the data center and hospital, to remote clinics, pharmacies, and even includes patient and care givers homes.

VMware SD-WAN is a key enabler for the delivery of the digital care and integrated systems, which can result in reduced healthcare costs, better quality of care, and operational transparency.

This chapter is focused on the following three constituents in the Healthcare industry:

- **Patients**- Individuals who receive medical care from providers

- **Providers**- Organizations that provide care to patients, charge payers for that care and procure health systems from vendors

- **Payers**- Organizations that pay providers for healthcare services, this includes insurance carriers, private employers, the government and individuals

Requirements: Delivering Superior Healthcare Outcomes

In order to meet the demands of a constantly changing landscape we must look at key aspects of what is needed to be successful. We will break down five key aspects any organizations need to take . into consideration.

Top imperatives for healthcare industry include:

- Enhancing the experience for external parties

- Improving internal processes and efficiency

- Security

- Cloud priorities

- Supporting innovative new healthcare opportunities

Enhancing the Experience for External Parties

As healthcare moves beyond the walls of the hospital, healthcare IT must reach beyond the data center. Patient experience is paramount for success and a key differentiator. A growing demand among patients for an enhanced service experience and greater participation in their care plan is placing further pressure on healthcare systems to find ways to become more patient-centered. This is where technology can play a crucial role delivering better outcomes and enabling brand recognition, which is a critical business outcome.

Healthcare providers depend on communication and collaboration to support every aspect of care, creating better experiences with patients and their families. Improving WAN performance and reliability can expedite patient admissions, improve collaboration with primary care physicians, specialists, and care team members resulting in higher quality care and patient satisfaction.

New technology trends such as bring-your-own-device (BYOD) initiatives and increasing mobility are also changing the way caregivers diagnose and treat their patients. It also enables clinical staff (doctors, nurses etc.) to be more collaborative and productive. For example, many healthcare providers are embracing a digital clinical workspace. A digital clinical workspace can incorporate a variety of devices, including Virtual Desktop Infrastructure (VDI), smart phones, and tablets, while providing the robust security demanded by the Health Insurance Portability and Accountability Act (HIPAA) and other regulations.

SD-WAN also provides better Business Continuity and Disaster Recovery (BC/DR) strategy offering organizations well defined policies supporting technical requirements of Healthcare Information and Management Systems Society (HIMSS) Stage 7[5].

The HIMSS Analytics Electronic Medical Record Adoption Model (EMRAM) incorporates methodology and algorithms to automatically score hospitals around the world relative to their Electronic Medical Records (EMR) capabilities. *This eight-stage (0-7) model measures the adoption and utilization of electronic medical record (EMR) functions. Move your organization closer to achieving a near paperless environment that harnesses technology to support optimized patient care by completing each stage below.*

5 "Stage 7" https://www.himssanalytics.org/emram

Most Electronic health record (EMR) applications are delivered through VMware Horizon published apps, view desktops or other similar desktop technologies. Virtual Desktop Infrastructure (VDI) centralizes all data and allows for more rigid access controls. Clinics are also transforming as there is more real time decision making (IoT, medical devices).

Better ways of understanding patient behavior leveraging cameras, sensors, wearable devices, Machine Learning and Artificial Intelligence (ML/AI) are generating considerable rich application content with the need to be connected in a highly available and secure way. This also leads to consistency of data across providers and their affiliates giving patient more flexibility and control.

However, these benefits come at the expense of higher bandwidth requirement/consumption, requiring a higher quality network to deliver an excellent experience for users.

Onsite at healthcare facilities, mobile technology, cameras, sensors and tablets paired with VDI and other applications can boost agility for caregivers who are on the move. They can provide rapid access to information, as well as help leverage the expertise of other colleagues, to enable healthcare providers to serve patients faster and deliver better outcomes.

55% of healthcare IT uses some form of Desktop as a Service (DaaS) or VDI.[6]

Improving Internal Processes and Efficiency

Increasingly, providers are utilizing electronic medical records/electronic health records (EMR/EHR) together with cloud-based healthcare solutions. Healthcare providers are mostly focused on EHR integration, mobile adoption, and physician buy-in. Healthcare companies are also looking at possible integration between EHR and patient generated data from mobile applications and wearables. Providers are still validating impact and value of integrating this unstructured data with EHR data. Though most health systems have an EHR system, EHR system optimization is still a huge focus for top executives. This is also giving providers an opportunity to be a EHR service provider for affiliates, small providers and private doctors. All these trends put a lot of stress on reliable connectivity which has intelligence to differentiate and prioritize traffic. This close integration sets the stage for many different benefits, including effortless sharing of data and of e-prescriptions. Always

6 LoginVSI https://info.loginvsi.com/acton/attachment/25205/f-0121/1/-/-/-/-/State%20of%20the%20VDI%20and%20SBC%20Survey%202017%20Edition%20v2.1.pdf?sid=TV2:g4MGwTlJe

accessible records also make it much easier for staff to access records, bills, and patient health insurance plans. Government security regulations are constantly evolving, and the threat landscape can change fast.

86.9% of physicians are using EMR/EHR systems [7]

Security

Security has been seen more focus and scrutiny in Healthcare. The last few years have seen an increase in data breaches and a rising value of stolen medical record information, further incentivizing bad actors. As healthcare becomes more distributed with applications moving from private data centers to public data centers and the expansion of healthcare systems into remote and rural facilities, there is more emphasis on secure communications.

As access to healthcare IT systems grow so too does the threat, and expanding access has the potential to lead to a larger attack surface. In addition to this, value-based care and population health management have broadened the data sharing environment, which adds more points of vulnerability as information enters and exits various portals, inboxes, and data warehouses. Healthcare providers and payers see that data sharing with third-parties is one of their biggest areas of concern. Compliance with regulations are required to avoid increased penalties with data breaches and building brand recognition. With this it is critical that patient data is encrypted in transit and Healthcare IT look at ways to segment patient related data traffic from all other traffic.

Cloud Priorities

Healthcare IT and developers are taking advantage of cloud providers extension of services and locations. This has moved healthcare's focus from when we will adopt a cloud solution, to how can it be done today. Healthcare providers and payers are realizing that their core business function is not building private data centers, and for certain applications public cloud is a better solution. Companies are leveraging SaaS applications like Salesforce (CRM), Lawson (ERP) and office 365. ESG data reveals that 89% of healthcare organizations currently use some form of public cloud service, whether SaaS, IaaS, or PaaS.

To meet these evolving requirements, many healthcare companies are embarking on digital transformation initiatives to deliver the appropriate workflows, policies, processes, and IT environments to provide a better experience to their customers. Electronic medical records, access to cloud-based applications, and connected IoT devices are all enabling healthcare professionals to provide higher levels of services. ESG research shows that the most important

7 https://www.cdc.gov/nchs/fastats/electronic-medical-records.htm

considerations for healthcare when justifying IT investments are improved customer satisfaction (35%), improved security (31%), and increased employee productivity (31%)[8].

Supporting Innovative, New Healthcare Opportunities

New initiatives like telehealth are putting quality care within reach even for people in rural locations. Video conferencing solutions enable healthcare providers to connect face to face with patients in rural areas, as well as elderly and disabled people—all in real time.

This is a great use case of how delivery of healthcare is going beyond the walls of hospitals and clinics. This is reducing healthcare costs and increases quality of care as patients don't need to wait in lines.

Telehealth enables access to primary care physicians and specialists regardless of their location. Providers can reach rural areas and provide reliable quality patient care and grow their members.

Increasingly, doctors and specialists are collaborating over the Internet to share and discuss high-resolution patient scans, test results, and other rich data. Robust, assured WAN performance is key to making such collaboration possible and effective.

Telemedicine is expected to grow to $40 billion by 2021.[9]

As per Orbis research, "Telemedicine market is projected to grow at a CAGR of 16.76% over the forecast period to reach US$48.985 billion by 2021, from the current estimate of $19.336 billion. Telemedicine market has been witnessing a high growth due to increasing government expenditure in healthcare, favorable industry regulations, focus towards privacy and the new trend of personal healthcare."

Challenges: Scale and Deliver Applications in the Cloud

As Healthcare embarks on its transformation journey, it also faces challenges with status quo. Providers contend with several challenges in their efforts to extend the reach of their healthcare offerings and better integrate it with cloud systems.

---

8 https://www.vmware.com/content/dam/digitalmarketing/vmware/en/pdf/products/vmw-positive-impact-sd-wan-healthcare-esg-whitepaper.pdf

9 "Telemedicine to reach $40B by 2021" https://www.reuters.com/brandfeatures/venture-capital/article?id=29410

Many organizations are backhauling Internet traffic to datacenters and paying a performance penalty for their cloud-based applications. They are purchasing expensive routers and paying high support costs to maintain remote healthcare locations. MPLS based circuits are expensive when compared to the cost of commercial and consumer broadband and takes lot of time to be provisioned, in rural areas MPLS circuit availability is also a major concern.

At the same time, their available Internet connections are often unreliable or provide poor performance. There is more integration happening between providers and payers, M&A's (Mergers and acquisitions) and integrating on-premise solutions with cloud-based solutions which takes time and resources. Healthcare providers are heavily investing in Ambulatory care or outpatient care, urgent care facilities as it offers higher premium and an avenue to add members, which means they need to a robust, cost effective and scalable solutions. IoT and medical devices on rise which needs to be connected and managed.

To keep pace with changing needs and support more innovative healthcare services, these firms need a WAN solution that will:

- Transport independent WAN, which can work with MPLS/Broadband/LTE/4G

- Meet industry compliance standards including HIPAA and PCI

- Patient information is protected and segmented

- Maximize network uptime to provide access to critical applications like EMR, radiology, pharmacy, claims etc

- Deliver high quality experience for Realtime applications like Telemedicine that leverage voice and video

- Simplified WAN management and operations

- Provide visibility, insight and control over application awareness and QoS.

- Improve failover processes to mitigate brownouts and blackout WAN conditions.

- Prioritize traffic over available bandwidth.

Solution: Simplified Architecture, Assured Performance Enhance Patient Outcomes

VMware SD-WAN by VeloCloud provides a flexible, secure, enterprise-grade solution for delivering assured performance that optimizes bandwidth and traffic prioritization to fit the specific needs of EHR and other healthcare applications. They can also establish a dependable network foundation to support advanced cloud applications and other critical application at data center sites that help enhance patient outcomes. VMware SD-WAN lets providers:

- Simplify WAN management with centralized, managed service monitoring and administration.

- Deliver transport-independent performance for the most demanding applications.

- Leverage bandwidth more economically with low-cost circuits and infrastructure.

- Provide a managed on-ramp to the cloud with performance, security and reliability.

- Business Policy Based Traffic Redirection & Service Insertion

- Get nonstop visibility and better insight into network health and performance.

Application and Data Segmentation

To help ensure that critical healthcare applications deliver the highest possible performance and security, VMware SD-WAN supports application and data segmentation. Healthcare providers can segment payments, patient records, IoT devices, corporate and Internet traffic, prioritize certain traffic over others by utilizing simple enterprise-wide segment creation capabilities. They can configure segment-aware policies and topologies for traffic both on-premises and in the cloud to help maintain compliance and security, while optimizing performance. *When you think about segmentations, it's about data sensitivity and location.*

Segmentation is also critical in Mergers & Acquisitions (M&A) or partnerships between providers and payers. Complexity is introduced because M&A sites already have their own connectivity in place. In a typical networking environment, the parent company may have to rip and replace existing circuits and infrastructure in the M&A sites to be integrated into the parent company. This process is often disruptive, technical difficult and slow, which often leads to disrupted services and dissatisfied physicians and care team members. Similarly, when there are partnerships and affiliates, healthcare staff (doctors, nurses, residents etc.) needs to visit affiliates facilities and work out of their premise.

These care givers need to access to both their organizations data as well as systems and date of the organization they are visiting, which poses a lot of challenge on how we segment traffic and still provide access to ensure employees can do their job.

With SD-WAN, healthcare organizations are able to extend their network architecture into the newly acquired sites by deploying edges and with zero touch provisioning (ZTP), adding them into the centralized management and orchestration portal.

Healthcare organizations can configure multiple enterprise-wide segments with just a few clicks (Figure 3.1).

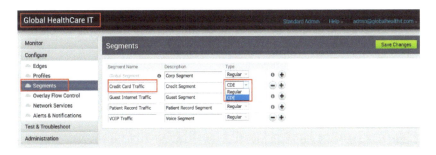

Figure 3.1 VMware SD-WAN by VeloCloud Enterprise-Wide Segment Configuration.

In this example, an enterprise administrator from Global Healthcare IT has configured segments for credit card application traffic, guest Internet, and other segments.

The "Credit Card Traffic" segment has been configured to only transmit through Cardholder Data Environment (CDE) earmarked gateways, limiting transactions to a secure, robust set of infrastructure components. When applied to the enterprise backbone, these segments have their own topologies, business policy, and firewall rule.

Furthermore, you can extend network segmentation from your remote locations (clinics/hospitals/medical office buildings (MoB)/offices etc.) to data center by integrating SD-WAN solution with VMware NSX data center. (Figure 3.2)

Edge to Edge Consistency and Security in Healthcare

Figure 3.2 VMware SD-WAN integration with NSX data center

To support an additional location, enterprise-wide provisioned segments can be extended on an individual basis to VMware SD-WAN Edges at the click of a button.

Within each segment, administrators have the ability to configure different polices as well as logic topologies on how traffic is directed through the overlay (Figure 3.3).

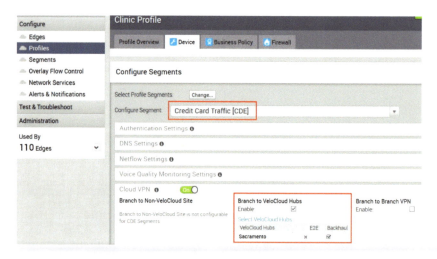

Figure 3.3 Configuring Segments with Separate VPN Topology (Non VeloCloud Site: NVS) Settings Applied to multiple Clinic Sites.

For organizations that choose to employ a cloud access security broker (CASB) for additional security, it is no longer necessary to build individual IPSec tunnels from each branch to the CASB provider (Figure 3.4). Instead, with VMware SD-WAN, traffic destined to the CASB provider is aggregated through a redundant set of cloud gateways to ease deployment.

Newly-provisioned sites that are attached to the profile will immediately be able to redirect traffic to the CASB provider as configured in the profile. With a single click, the provider can apply these configurations to multiple clinic sites.

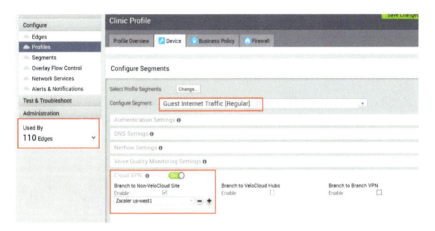

Figure 3.4 Guest Segment with Non-VeloCloud Site (NVS), a CASB Provider

Assured Application Performance and VDI Support

VMware SD-WAN enables organizations to set up and ensure assured application performance and appropriate traffic prioritization over any link, whether MPLS or Internet broadband. The solution supports continuous monitoring, dynamic per-packet steering, and on-demand remediation to maximize performance for latency-sensitive healthcare applications and media.

For organizations utilizing VDI applications or patient records software, the solution provides intuitive tools to configure rules and prioritize critical applications with just a few clicks. For example, VMware Horizon View™ delivers desktop services from the cloud to enable end-user freedom, together with IT management and control. By default, VMware SD-WAN recognizes the most common VDI applications available (Figure 3.5).

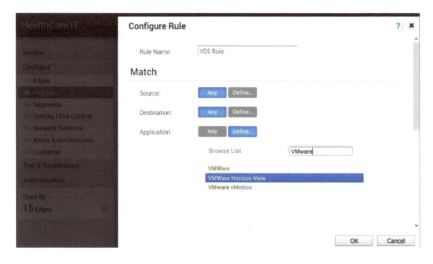

Figure 3.5 VMware SD-WAN Business Policy with Common VDI Application.

Zero-Touch Deployment Agility

For growing healthcare organizations, VMware SD-WAN supports simple, quick deployment and delivers zero-touch agility. Healthcare providers can quickly install and provision new sites with no IT visit required and no pre-staging. Additionally, no site-by-site link knowledge is necessary. To bring up a new site, a network administrator can simply create a configuration and send an email with activation key to the installer. A non-technical local employee can power up the VMware SD-WAN Edge, connect it to the Internet, then click on the activation key to activate the device. Internet connectivity can also act as a backup link in this type of deployment.

Improve Visibility and Management

With VMware SD-WAN, healthcare providers can utilize a centralized, cloud-based orchestrator to gain better visibility and understanding of the state of their network. At the same time, healthcare providers have the flexibility to employ all solution components on-premises. Potential issues can be automatically discovered in real time and, using on-demand remediation, VMware SD-WAN reduces impact on service and performance. Improved network uptime means improved ability to treat patients, for better outcomes and a more satisfying overall experience.

Healthcare SD-WAN Use Cases

Extending EMR Community Access

Quickly Enable Urgent & Ambulatory Care

Tele Medicine/ Tele Health

Seamless Mergers & Acquisitions

End to End Segmentation

Figure 3.6 Showcasing Healthcare SD-WAN Use Cases

In Focus: Healthcare Provider can be service providers offering their services to small providers, affiliates (community connect)

Healthcare organizations are actively extending their services out to affiliate clinics and hospitals. The reason for this change is due to Mergers and Acquisitions, partnership and organizations becoming service providers. Hospital System extends EMR and other services from their parent site to a remote facility. Independent physician groups are seeking to partner with larger organizations in a bid to stay independent, while lowering cost, and modernizing their care delivery though an EMR. Organizations have difficulty supporting these affiliates sites and the various hardware they own, while maintaining SLAs. It can take weeks or even months for a carrier to make available a leased MPLS line to connect a new remote office. It is difficult to predict the onboarding outcome when working with so many different organizations. The result is often missed deadlines and potentially improper configuration, resulting in delays in patient care, lost revenue, and unhappy care providers.

As mentioned earlier most of those EMR applications are delivered through Horizon Published apps, Desktops, or other similar products. With care providers spending most of their onscreen time interacting with the published application, VMware SD-WAN will be configured for application-aware Per-packet steering. Administrators can create Business Policies for their EMR to always prefer the MPLS connection and to ensure it has the largest share of the preferred connection.

Figure 3.7 VMware SD-WAN connectivity from Remote Clinic to Hospital

In this configuration, we leverage traffic steering on the broadband connection to send other EMR traffic such as reporting activity done by analysts, printing traffic, and any other non-patient facing traffic. In the event of failure of either link, VMware SD-WAN DMPO (Dynamic Multi-Path Optimization) will dynamically ensure the clinical application and care provider workflows are preferred as per business policies.

VMware Dynamic Multi-path Optimization (DMPO) enables application-aware dynamic per-packet steering, on-demand remediation and overlay Quality of Service; DMPO ensures optimal SD-WAN performance for the most demanding applications over any transport (Internet or Hybrid) and any destination (On-Premises or Cloud).

Business Policies are very powerful as they abstract the underlying WAN interface, device type or WAN carrier giving consistent policies across enterprise. Every clinical site will have same EMR business policy independent of WAN carrier type, link type and interface type.

In Focus: Healthcare Provider Maximizes Reliability and Meets Privacy Regulations

A major healthcare provider in Texas relies on information technology to help diagnose, treat, and bill its patients. Like many healthcare companies, the provider has moved its billing systems and patient records to the cloud. The cloud provides patients the flexibility to be treated at any location, and lets doctors evaluate patients regardless of where they are working. The stakes are high, because any network downtime can impact patient treatment and outcomes, as well as compromise healthcare regulations like HIPAA.

The provider was using broadband links to connect dozens of healthcare locations, with small firewall appliances in place at each branch. Its existing system lacked application awareness and could not measure line quality. If a primary line was not working well, a resulting brownout could potentially impact performance on all medical applications across its network.

The provider needed a better way to optimize the performance and reliability of its cloud-based applications and ensure compliance with privacy regulations.

After evaluating several options, the provider chose VMware SD-WAN by VeloCloud, featuring the VMware SD-WAN Orchestrator for centralized management, monitoring, and changes, as well as VMware SD-WAN Edges at each branch on the network.

The solution offers:

- **Consistent, dependable performance:** Superior infrastructure performance helps ensure the provider can treat patients and access records at all times, for better compliance and outcomes.

- **Fast and seamless solution deployment:** To bring up a new branch location, on-site employees can simply plug in the VMware SD-WAN Edge device— with no expensive, specialized truck rolls required.

- **Continuous visibility and visualization:** In-depth insight into network performance helps network teams identify and remediate any issue before it impacts users, as well as capturing historical performance records of network behavior.

The solution also offers the Quality of Service (QoS) required to deploy the latest VoIP applications across its entire network. The solution can scale easily to accommodate new initiatives such as an EMR to help manage the care of its patients.

In Focus: Telemedicine Professionals Scale Collaboration

A leading telemedicine firm offers an array of medical imaging services through a team of radiologists, technologists, IT and research specialists, and other professionals. With 25 freestanding imaging centers across seven states, the firm serves hundreds of physicians and medical centers.

Collaboration is key to supporting patients that see different specialists for different medical conditions. To deliver the best possible patient outcome, each provider needs secure, rapid access to individual patient data, regardless of location.

To deliver this access, the telemedicine firm needed a secure, flexible network infrastructure that would enable it to send and receive patient data across its imaging centers throughout the U.S.

After exploring several alternatives, the firm deployed VMware SD-WAN, making it easy for branch sites to securely share patient data with one another, and with external medical providers through an encrypted network. The solution delivers:

- **Support for bandwidth-intensive applications:** VMware SD-WAN helps ensure that the provider can deliver sufficient bandwidth leveraging link aggregation at each site to support increasing volumes of patient data. It enables organizations to not only send patient data to its healthcare clients, but also receive patient data for medical imaging.

- **Collaborative ecosystem:** VMware SD-WAN provides the rich infrastructure necessary to support collaboration among healthcare professionals nationwide. The solution also supports Network Service Chaining enabling Internet back-haul for ease of security policy and deployment.

- **Data integrity:** With its new system in place, the firm gains the confidence and assurance that its applications will seamlessly deliver their most valuable information with minimal risk.

- **Maximum uptime:** Network availability is an imperative in healthcare. VMware SD-WAN supports LTE failover to deliver critical healthcare information consistently and dependably.

VMware SD-WAN enables this leading Telemedicine provider to support its most mission- critical applications over a transport-agnostic, scalable infrastructure.

Before and After: The SD-WAN Difference

Traditional healthcare WAN environments often employ an active backup mode, with Internet links in standby mode not being used (Figure 3.7). Internet links employ IPSec tunnels from the clinic to headquarters. The IPSec- protected backup connections will only engage and carry patient data in the event of a catastrophic failure of the primary MPLS link. This means that the backup links use is inefficient and is unlikely to have the same network characteristics as on the MPLS link.

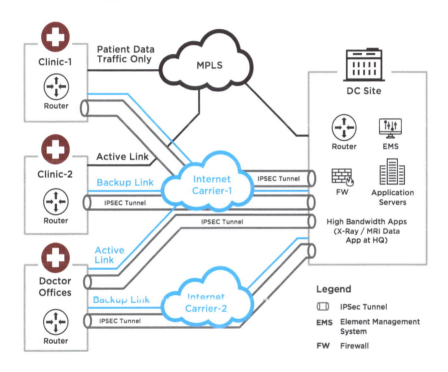

Figure 3.8 Healthcare Before SD-WAN

With VMware SD-WAN by VeloCloud, all links are active-active mode (Figure 3.8). A single overlay consists of multiple segments. Each segment can isolate guest, patient data, and VoIP traffic. With VMware SD-WAN overlay tunnel, all links are aggregated for higher bandwidth for bulk applications.

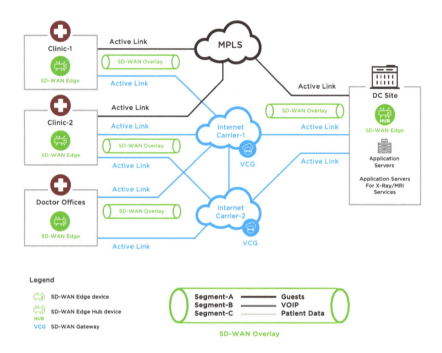

Figure 3.9 Healthcare with VMware SD-WAN

What You Need to Know

- Enterprise-grade VMware SD-WAN by VeloCloud lets healthcare providers deliver secure, consistent application performance to patients and staff at any location.

- For organizations utilizing VDI applications, VMware SD-WAN offers intuitive tools to configure rules and prioritize critical applications with just a few clicks.

- Assured application performance over any link, whether MPLS, Internet broadband, or LTE circuits, helps minimize outages and improve efficiency and outcomes.

- Simple enterprise-wide segment creation lets providers segment payments, patient records, Internet traffic, and more.

- Digital Health connect providing seamless, secure and scalable connectivity.

Chapter 4

Forging Stronger Customer Connections in Retail

Retail organizations face distinct challenges in their efforts to deliver a superior experience to every customer, regardless of how, where, and when they are shopping. In this chapter, we will discuss how VMware SD-WAN by VeloCloud helps retailers better engage customers and enhance profitability.

Requirements: Meeting Omnichannel Expectations in Retail

In an increasingly mobile, digital world, consumers have more choices than ever in terms of how, where, and when they shop. Retailers are under constant pressure to deliver a consistently outstanding omnichannel experience, compete more effectively, and boost profitability.

Shoppers expect an engaging, personalized experience, whether they are browsing in person or digitally. To deliver an omnichannel experience, retailers are turning to the cloud, mobile, artificial intelligence (AI), augmented reality, and other transformative technologies. They are seeking better ways to track every consumer's journey; analyze and apply customer data for better insights; and deliver the right information at the right time—whether online, mobile, or in a store.

For example, AI applications help clothing retailers better understand customers' behavior and personal preferences; anticipate their needs and purchases; and deliver a more engaging overall experience. AI and augmented reality can support intelligent smart mirrors to let consumers "try on" outfits virtually, before they purchase them, and support dynamic, streamlined loyalty programs.

Retailers are also employing these advanced technologies to better understand and engage consumers. Analytics and AI are helping them provide the relevant, context-rich content they need. They can support compelling retail offerings like coupons and promotional offers that shoppers can receive on their smart phones as they shop or automate complementary product suggestions in real time.

According to Forbes, with 6.4 Billion IoT devices currently and an expectation of more than 50 billion by 2020, all of the data that is being produced from our "Things" will become high impact consumption data that retailers will be able to utilize to personalize shopping experiences and put the right products in front of the right people at the right time.[10]

Digital transformation provides a compelling opportunity for retailers, but it also requires tremendous bandwidth, especially for media-rich content such as video. Retail organizations require a scalable, flexible infrastructure that can provide the performance and availability they need to support an emerging wave of exciting new applications, as well as long-standing requirements like secure credit card transactions.

---

10 "Top Five Digital Transformation Trends in Retail," Daniel Newman, Forbes, March 2017.

Challenges: Overcoming Limitations to Deliver a World-Class Retail Experience

Retailers understand that they must engage customers better on every channel to stay competitive, but all too often, their existing infrastructures are holding them back. They have limited resources and scaling those resources to hundreds or even thousands of retail locations is very challenging. At the same time, retailers must keep costs in check and increase operational efficiencies, so they can compete more effectively and do more with less.

To deliver the superior experience customers expect, retailers need a versatile, secure platform that can support their most critical applications and services—regardless of location. It must:

- **Deliver the right performance on the right application:** To successfully support omnichannel interaction, retailers must manage and prioritize traffic for a variety of applications, including video, wireless, VoIP, among others, providing the best possible performance on mobile phones, tablets, in-store kiosks, and other devices.

- **Secure and manage sales transactions:** Retailers must securely manage a variety of point-of-sale (POS) transactions in-store, online, and even from mobile shoppers. They need to make it fast and frictionless for consumers to shop, while maintaining security as well as meeting Payment Card Industry (PCI) compliance and other regulations.

- **Enable secure and reliable guest Internet access:** Today's tech-savvy shoppers often browse the Internet while shopping. According to Forbes, 82% of smart phone users check their phones in the store while deciding what to buy[11]. Retailers need to provide uninterrupted Internet browsing and the security required for safe guest access without compromising their own data and compliance.

- **Maximize system uptime for continuous revenue:** Even a short service interruption can impact revenues, frustrate consumers, and damage retailer reputations. Organizations need a solution that delivers high availability and complete insight and control. If a problem does arise, they need the confidence in knowing that they can quickly manage and resolve issues remotely, without sending a network team professional to a site.

---

11 "Top Five Digital Transformation Trends in Retail," Daniel Newman, Forbes, March 2017.

- **Do more in limited space:** Space is at a premium for retailers, most of whom have limited network closet space. They need small-footprint technology solutions that are efficient, easy to manage, and consume minimal power and resources. In pop-up store environments, all networking capabilities need to be delivered in a single form factor, because large equipment stacks are prohibitive.

Solution: Enhancing Interaction on Every Channel with VMware SD-WAN by VeloCloud

Flexible and secure, enterprise-grade VMware SD-WAN by VeloCloud enables retailers to overcome real-world limitations and deliver a delightful, engaging customer experience—however and wherever they are shopping. A single, manageable platform lets network teams add cost-effective Internet links without compromising control over optimal application access. It lets them aggregate multiple broadband links, such as LTE, or other transport to support cloud applications, real-time voice and video, and other latency-sensitive applications. This lets retailers serve customers in digital and physical environments consistently and cost-effectively. The solution offers:

- Internet as transport
- Quality of Experience (QoE)
- Compliance and security
- Traffic segmentation
- Efficient management

Let us take a closer look at the benefits retailers can unleash by accelerating digital transformation with SD-WAN.

Internet as Transport

VMware SD-WAN enables secure and reliable connectivity over any transport type. What happens when retailers migrate to a more agile, flexible infrastructure foundation? They unlock dramatic savings in capital expenses (CapEx) and operational expenses (OpEx) by reducing complexity and space requirements, while increasing efficiency. Retailers can set up broadband connections much faster and at a lower cost than private links. They no longer need to purchase links based on the function they provide, such as providing access to corporate applications at the data center or access the Internet for guest services. Corporate applications and other offerings can be accessed over the Internet-based overlay network. At the same time, enhancing operational efficiency frees up network teams to focus on more strategic business concerns.

Quality of Experience

Increasing consumer expectations for fast, personalized services, together with escalating bandwidth and performance requirements within stores and properties, are pushing retailers to deliver services faster and more efficiently. Retailers have to ensure applications can be accessed with the same efficiency, no matter where they're located.

VMware SD-WAN enables retailers to enhance the service level, performance, and capacity of broadband Internet links as well as hybrid networks. Dynamic Multi-Path Optimization technology, together with deep application recognition, aggregates multiple links and steers traffic over the most optimal links to ensure a consistent and reliable user experience. Secure and reliable connectivity between retail locations can be facilitated by VMware SD-WAN Edges located at each retail location, without having to traverse the datacenter. Cloud and Internet access is enabled by connecting VMware SD-WAN Edges at each of the retail locations to global VMware SD-WAN Gateways.

Blackouts are rare threats in retail, but still pose a problem when they occur (Figure 4.1). If a link failure takes place, sessions to SaaS applications routinely get interrupted, because the outbound source IP address of the flow changes when it is moved to a new link. The Dynamic Multi-Path Optimization overlay can preserve this address. It can also ensure that the flow can be moved in a sub-second fashion compared to traditional multi-minute convergence times that are expected from routing protocols.

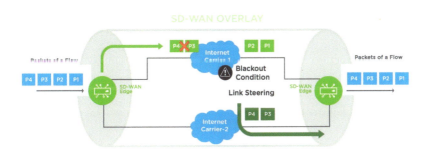

Figure 4.1 VMware SD-WAN Dynamic Multi-Path Optimization Blackout Protection

To minimize brownouts, the VMware SD-WAN can dynamically duplicate packets for real-time flows when packet loss above threshold is detected (Figure 4.2). It can leverage multiple links (if available) to duplicate packets.

The receiving VCE takes the first packet that arrives and discards any duplicates.

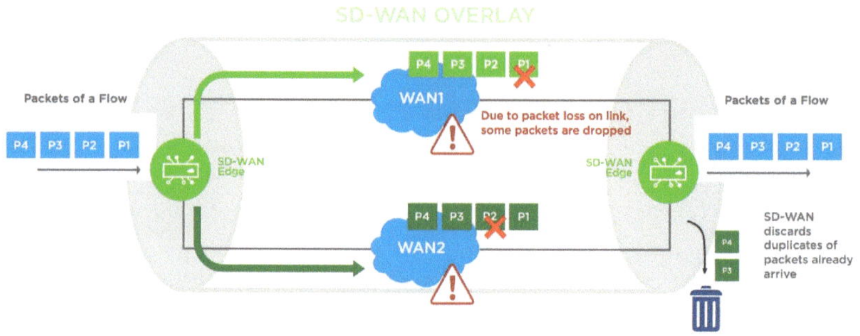

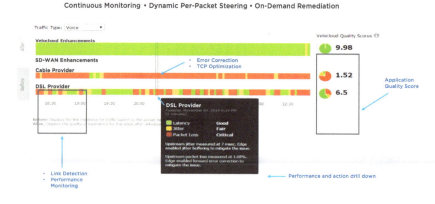

Figure 4.2 VMware SD-WAN Dynamic Multi-Path Optimization Brownout Protection

A quality score is measured by the VMware SD-WAN Edges and reported to the Orchestrator (Figure 4.3). It shows the quality of the individual underlays, as well as the SD-WAN overlay, and provides insight into any impairment that occurred, and how the system reacted to remediate it.

Dynamic Multi-Path Optimization remediates the effects on the end-user experience by employing link steering, forward error correction and de-jitter buffering measures. The end result, marked "After," shows a sanitized overlay network where the business-critical applications are no longer impacted by the impaired underlays.

Figure 4.3 VMware SD-WAN Dynamic Multi-Path Optimization Optimizes Application Performance over Broadband Links.

It is important to point out that routing protocols only will act in the event of a blackout condition were the active transport link becomes disconnected. Brownout conditions where minor ongoing packet loss occurs on the transport, impacting end user experience, are not detected by the routing protocol, and are more difficult to troubleshoot.

Compliance and Security

Retail firms depend on credit card payments for many of their core business functions. That's why it is important to choose a SD-WAN solution that is not only PCI-compliant, but also facilitates simplification of the PCI audit process.

The Payment Card Industry Data Security Standard (PCI-DSS) is a worldwide information security standard, provided by the PCI Security Standards Council, that helps organizations safeguard the processing of credit card payments and prevent fraud. The VMware SD-WAN network lets organizations protect cardholder data, implement strong access control and change management measures, and monitor network security.

VMware SD-WAN helps retail organizations achieve PCI compliance in a simple, efficient and cost-effective manner. Retailers can work through PCI audits by employing PCI as a Service and separate credit card traffic with segmentation.

Retailers and service providers can establish their own PCI-compliant environments with VMware SD-WAN. Network teams can leverage VMware SD-WAN Attestation of Compliance (AoC) to simplify and accelerate their own PCI audit process (Figure 4.4)

Ensure PCI compliance in a simple, efficient, and cost-effective manner

The first and only solution to offer PCI-Certified Cloud-Delivered SD-WAN

All VMware SD-WAN by VeloCloud components are PCI Compliant

Retailers benefit from VMware SD-WAN by VeloCloud PCI AOC to simplify PCI Audit

VMware SD-WAN by VeloCloud is a PCI DSS (v3.2) Level 1 Service Provider

Figure 4.4 VMware SD-WAN Business Policy with Common VDI Application.

The VMware SD-WAN Orchestrator provides centralized visibility and management that enables geographically distributed organizations to set up PCI-compliant architectures across large numbers of retail locations.

Traffic Segmentation

VMware SD-WAN enables traffic segmentation that is critical for retailers who must isolate different types of traffic while maintaining specific business policies. For example, if regulations mandate segregation of sensitive PCI credit card traffic from corporate traffic and guest Internet traffic, organizations can apply it to comply with these requirements.

With VMware SD-WAN, retailers can easily create separate, distinct VPN topologies, firewall and business rules to separate traffic as they wish, as previously discussed. They can direct all guest Wi-Fi traffic to a secure gateway or firewall, while running voice traffic between sites over a dynamic secure link between retail locations. VMware SD-WAN supports automated firewall and VPN rules for each segment, across the network and cloud.

Segments can be used to strictly segregate network use between different business units in an organization (Figure 4.5). These segments are automatically extended over the SD-WAN overlay and can provide access to different environments in the datacenter.

Organizations can also employ segmentation to isolate guest traffic from corporate applications and resources. Each segment has its own unique topology, as well as completely independent application priority and security policies. In this example, social networking applications are blocked for the PCI segment, but are allowed on the guest segment.

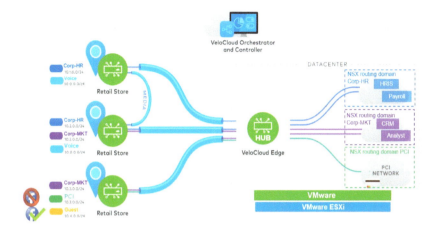

Figure 4.5 VMware SD-WAN Segmentation

VMware SD-WAN also helps retail organizations address external security threats with a stateful, context-aware firewall for applications, users, and devices. With support for one-click VPN for retail-to-datacenter and retail-cloud traffic, the solution can scale efficiently across thousands of retail locations.

VMware SD-WAN can also enable security services as a Virtual Network Function (VNF) to operate inline on VMware SD-WAN Edge devices hardware, making it an ideal solution for environments where space is limited, and power or cooling budgets are tight or where device consolidation is necessary. This also facilitates managing multiple services from a single management portal – the VMware SD-WAN Orchestrator, delivering continued simplicity.

Efficient Management

Like most organizations, retailers accumulate new infrastructure components, connections, and services over time. VMware SD-WAN helps reduce point products and provides uniform management across the network and improves insight and visibility into every branch. Network teams gain centralized management control, for faster, more proactive troubleshooting across all their retail locations. Centralized, efficient management also helps them get more from limited resources.

VMware SD-WAN also lets organizations take advantage of zero-touch deployment and automation capabilities, for fast, plug-and-play deployment. Activation, configuration, and ongoing management are all handled in the cloud, without requiring expensive IT professionals onsite. When it's time to apply a new policy, a single click can distribute it across all retail locations through a centralized, cloud-based orchestrator.

VMware SD-WAN can create a dynamic inventory for all sites and connected links. It can provide details on link quality performance of connected providers by location, to deliver performance insight and metrics.

Let's take a closer look at how a variety of retail firms have transformed their operations with VMware SD-WAN.

In Focus: Global Clothing Retailer Delivers A Superior Customer Experience as it Grows

A major global clothing retailer with more than 500 locations worldwide faced changing customer needs and challenges as the company expanded. The firm was committed to delivering the best possible service to customers, both in-store and online, but was unsure if its existing infrastructure could keep pace with growing demands.

To compete more effectively, the retailer decided to transform its network to build a dynamic, responsive, efficient organization. The retailer's in-house staff of network teams was small, so simple deployment and management was key.

After evaluating a variety of options, the clothing retailer migrated its retail locations from a traditional WAN environment to VMware SD-WAN. Installation was simple, and no downtime was required. Stores that were at the end of their private link contracts were converted to a broadband Internet connection and the VMware SD-WAN Edge was installed on-premises. Most sites were up and running within an hour. With its new SD-WAN solution in place, the clothing retailer is realizing:

- **Nonstop transaction readiness:** Under the previous architecture, a network outage made it impossible for a retail location to process sales. With VMware SD-WAN, if the primary broadband connection fails, traffic can be immediately rerouted over an LTE backup, for maximum business continuity.

- **Fast, efficient location launches:** Instead of waiting for days or weeks for a carrier to install a new circuit, the retailer can apply a pre-set store profile and have its VMware SD-WAN Edge device operational within minutes.

- **Dependable in-store online browsing:** For customers that have a special clothing requirement that is not available in-store, the retailer offers on-site online ordering, delivering the bandwidth and performance customers need for an optimal buying experience.

- **Support for Voice over IP (VoIP):** The solution enables the firm to modernize its phone system by migrating sites to VoIP without the need for additional switches, reducing the hardware footprint at each location.

With VMware SD-WAN, this innovative retailer can take advantage of increased network performance and improved visibility, as well as offer a superior consumer experience.

In Focus: Flooring Distributor Builds a More Agile, Expandable Organization on the Cloud

A leading distributor of tile, carpet, and other flooring supplies was facing competitive pressure and growing pains. Its network team was seeking to integrate disparate company networks and platforms, speed time to market, and develop an infrastructure that would better scale to meet growing customer needs.

With 25 locations, the firm knew that its reliance on its legacy network would impede its ability to achieve this integration and put a significant burden on the network team. The firm was also seeking to minimize redundancy and move beyond its costly, limited MPLS network.

Working closely with an SD-WAN partner, the distributor deployed VMware SD-WAN, including VMware SD-WAN Edges at each location to connect to the cloud using the VMware SD-WAN Gateway. The solution also used VMware SD-WAN Orchestrator for complete network visibility and centralized management. VMware SD-WAN delivered:

- **Support for cloud applications and services:** VMware SD-WAN enabled a fast, secure connection to all locations, enabling the distributor to move more of its services to the cloud. The firm has also deployed VoIP throughout its sites for additional savings and improved communications.

- **Rapid deployments:** Opening new locations became fast and easy. With VMware SD-WAN, the flooring distributor was able to establish connectivity quickly at any location, with any available connection.

- **Serious cost savings:** Migrating from its existing MPLS environment has enabled the distributor to save hundreds of thousands of dollars per year by taking advantage of inexpensive broadband links, more proactive management, and rich cloud capabilities.

VMware SD-WAN enables the flooring distributor to enhance visibility and improve security of its POS transactions, prioritizing PCI traffic over non-critical data, to serve customers more efficiently and securely.

Before and After: The SD-WAN Difference

Without an SD-WAN, retailers employed multiple devices at store locations, such as firewalls, routers, and wireless access points (Figure 4.6). Each of these devices required separate element management. Retailers had to manage multiple devices on branch sites, facing complex troubleshooting and deployment, along with ongoing multi-vendor support requirements. Segments had to be created individually on per-link basis.

Retailers employed separate IPSec tunnels for each traffic type such as PCI transactions and guest traffic, on public links. They often configured separate virtual LANs (VLANs) on MPLS links as well.

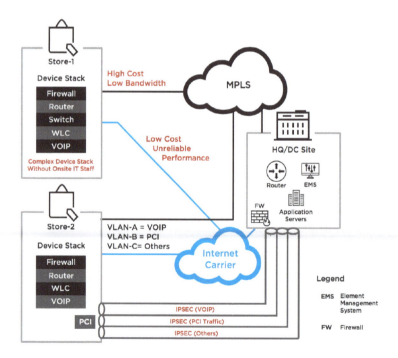

Figure 4.6 Retail Before SD-WAN

VMware SD-WAN lets retailers enjoy simple, faster deployment for store locations with an all in one VMware SD-WAN Edge device (Figure 4.7). Applications can be moved to the cloud and can be accessed from VMware SD-WAN Gateway. These cloud applications are protected and optimized by VMware SD-WAN Dynamic Multi-Path Optimization.

VMware SD-WAN also lets stores use multiple Internet links for reliability. All the links are active-active (private and public links). Retailers can send all the traffic to SD-WAN overlay tunnel, and all links can be used for business-critical traffic. With VMware SD-WAN segmentation, a single overlay can carry all the segment's traffic. These segments can be understood by the datacenter site with a VMware SD-WAN Edge device.

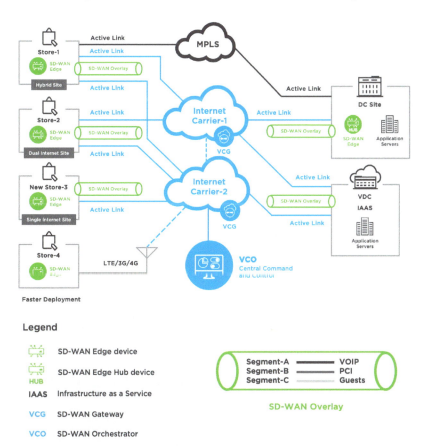

Figure 4.7 Connecting Retail Locations with VMware SD-WAN

What You Need to Know

- With VMware SD-WAN, retail organizations deliver an engaging, enjoyable omnichannel experience to every customer, every time.

- Dynamic Multi-Path Optimization enhances application performance and enables seamless failover connections for WAN.

- VMware SD-WAN lets retail organizations simplify and streamline operations with centralized management, maximizing uptime and helping network teams get the most from limited resources.

- Retailers can benefit from PCI compliant VMware SD-WAN components for secure credit card payments. Segmentation allows separation of credit card, guest, and corporate retail traffic, with different topologies and distinct application and firewall rules for each segment.

Chapter 5

Building Customer Loyalty in the Hospitality Sector

Like most organizations, hospitality organizations are reconsidering the way they do business in a more connected, mobile world. VMware SD-WAN provides the foundation to help them keep pace in a highly competitive industry.

Requirements: Delivering a Delightful Guest Experience in Hospitality

Digital transformation is driving new challenges for hospitality firms. Like retailers, hospitality firms must provide a frictionless, enjoyable experience to consumers with high expectations. In today's hyperconnected world, providing a great Internet connection can be just as important as a hotel's location.

Guests are making reservations and interacting with properties via many different channels, including mobile, web, and phone systems.

Once at a property, guests demand access to rich media content and sophisticated communications options, such as guest Wi-Fi. They often need to support multiple connected user devices in a room. Even a brief network outage can impact the visitor experience.

To provide an experience and service level that will keep guests coming back, hotels and resorts require excellent connectivity both inside and outside their property. They need a robust Wi-Fi network for mobile users and guests, as well top-quality Internet connectivity, even during peak usage periods.

Hospitality companies also face constant pressure to do more with less, enhance productivity and efficiency, and stay out in front of competitors with constant innovation.

Challenges: Engage Guests and Keep Services Available

Dependable, high-performance connectivity is critical to providing a great customer experience, and the challenge will only grow. To compete effectively, hospitality firms need a platform that will:

- Extend easily and cost effectively across multiple properties, and scale when needs change.
- Deliver voice and Wi-Fi for guests and employees.
- Provide granular yet centralized control over applications and services.
- Minimize service outages for optimal guest experience.
- Protect and secure guest data.
- Provide segregated network segments for on-premises suppliers such as excursion reservation desks or photography services.

Solution: Serving Guests Better and More Efficiently

A scalable SD-WAN enables hospitality firms to deliver the services their employees and guests require, in a way that is fully manageable and scalable. VMware SD-WAN provides a business-quality framework to implement the rules they need for all their sites with just a few clicks and policy changes. The solution offers:

- **Simpler, faster location deployments:** With VMware SD-WAN, hospitality organizations can rapidly deploy and configure new services to new properties at the touch of a button. This requires less oversight from on-premises network staff.

- **Network-wide IP phone system:** VoIP capabilities are becoming more important as hospitality providers look to save money and provide richer voice communication services. VMware SD-WAN lets them do both.

- **Granular bandwidth and control:** VMware SD-WAN provides robust management to enable hospitality providers to scale when needs change, and prioritize demanding applications.

Simpler, Faster Location Deployments

Deploying technology to new locations can be slow and cumbersome for hospitality providers. Organizations must often manually configure each piece of hardware on-site, test connections, and then manage them independently from any other nodes on the network. Any changes might require an on-site technician.

VMware SD-WAN also gives hospitality companies access to a wide range of bandwidth choices, enabling them to mix and match service providers and ensure a highly resilient WAN. With easy access to multiple, widely-available broadband links, organizations can rapidly establish new links as soon as they are required.

VMware SD-WAN also helps hospitality organizations keep equipment footprint to a minimum in limited spaces. With VMware SD-WAN, new locations are easy to set up with VMware SD-WAN Edge. Because it is simple to use and deploy, trained technicians are not required (Figure 5.1). This small footprint also helps minimize complexity, consolidating all needed functionality into one, future-proof device. All configurations can be performed through the VMware SD-WAN Orchestrator.

1. Create Config & Send Key

IT Admin adds a new VeloCloud Edge in the customer account.

IT Admin generates an activation key and emails it to the Installer.

2. Device Ships

VeloCloud Edge with factory default config is shipped to the remote site.

Office Admin powers up the device and connects it to the Internet.

3. Install, Authenticate & Pull Config

Office Admin plugs in the device and connects to the Internet through VeloCloud Edge WLAN/LAN

Office admin clicks on activation link in the email. Edge is activated.

Figure 5.1 Zero-Touch Provisioning Enables Deployment in Minutes.

Network-wide IP Phone System

Phone systems are an integral part of the guest experience for many hospitality firms. However, dropped calls, latency, and jitter can frustrate visitors and employees.

VMware SD-WAN lets organizations route their voice traffic over an intelligent system that can offer secure and reliable connectivity in and out of each location, for clear, quality VoIP calls. Hospitality locations can save money on phone communications, while helping organizations avoid expensive investments in traditional and legacy PBX systems.

Granular Bandwidth Management and Scalability

Hospitality providers face escalating application demands and rapidly-changing tenants as events are scheduled in the property. Each event tenant or on-site activity provider will require a portion of the available bandwidth, and expect guarantees around its availability. During peak periods, bandwidth can get consumed quickly as the number of users on the network surges. To address the issue, they would traditionally purchase additional MPLS leased lines. Or they could increase Internet access capacity, depending on which options were available to them. Organizations could also apply Quality of Service (QoS) to extract improved performance from their available bandwidth. These options were often costly, required complex management, and could not always guarantee the right level of performance.

VMware SD-WAN provides the control and manageability needed to support today's changing expectations. With innovative technologies like Dynamic Multi-Path Optimization, hospitality providers can optimize application performance and enable seamless failover connections for WAN, for dependable delivery of voice, video, and other demanding application traffic. Moreover, VMware SD-WAN works with the hospitality provider's existing network and does not require a forklift upgrade. It is an ideal solution to augment existing MPLS networks with Internet links for added capacity.

Centralized management tools enable network teams to gain a deeper understanding into how their guests are consuming Internet services, and which applications they are running—and when. If an issue arises, these management capabilities make it easier to track down the cause and fix it faster.

With VMware SD-WAN, hospitality companies can deliver high-performance connectivity to their guests by augmenting all available public and private transport. If a property has a conference, training or similar event planned, they can easily allocate additional bandwidth for an influx of users. They also gain improved visibility into their entire network, to acquire better insight into how its services are being consumed.

In Focus: Growing Hospitality Provider Scales for Success

A hospitality firm based in California depends on its network to support growth and guest services. However, its existing MPLS WAN slowed deployment of new circuits, and was expensive to manage and maintain. Each location has its own retail system, and the network team is also supporting numerous Software-as-a-Service (SaaS) and cloud-based applications.

The company was seeking a solution that could help it reduce its cost of ownership, speed up acquisitions and expansions, and ensure a high-quality experience for its guests.

After considering a variety of options, the hospitality firm chose VMware SD-WAN to simplify its branch office networking, while assuring the best possible application performance. Its architecture supports remote management and operates smoothly across any combination of public or private circuits.

With VMware SD-WAN, the hospitality firm enjoys:

- **Accelerated acquisitions:** Now the firm can grow at its own pace, instead of taking months to wait for an MPLS circuit. With VMware SD-WAN, network teams can connect a new location in just a few days, with assured performance, quality, and availability. They could simply deploy an overlay over the existing infrastructure, making the resources of the acquired company available in a matter of hours.

- **A superior guest experience:** Rapid service delivery has enhanced the quality of network services at individual sites, making it easier for sales and marketing teams to entice new guests. VMware SD-WAN helps the hospitality firm differentiate itself with a consistently enjoyable visitor experience.

- **Simplified infrastructure and management:** Under its legacy infrastructure, each site had four to five network devices deployed. VMware SD-WAN has enabled many locations to replace disparate devices with just one, thanks to its integrated firewall and VPN features. Its centralized management supports zero-touch configuration, for simpler, more efficient management everywhere. VMware SD-WAN provides a single pane of glass view for the entire SD-WAN management.

With VMware SD-WAN, the hospitality firm has reduced bandwidth costs and can now provision new locations without truck rolls, which adds up to big time and expense savings.

Before and After: The SD-WAN Difference

Without SD-WAN, corporate applications like booking systems, digital signage, and other processes, are accessed using private links only (Figure 5.2). The Internet link is dedicated for guest access only.

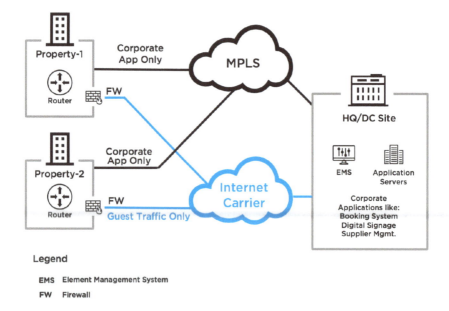

Legend

EMS Element Management System

FW   Firewall

Figure 5.2 Hospitality Before SD-WAN

With VMware SD-WAN, any links can be used for corporate traffic (Figure 5.3). SD-WAN overlay tunnel in public Internet can be used for corporate traffic. Internet traffic can also be constrained to use public links only.

VMware SD-WAN overlay can provide multiple segregated network segment for traffic such as PCI traffic can be isolated and directed to a payment card server, Guest wifi traffic could be directed to firewall or cloud security services. By leveraging VMware SD-WAN segmentation, network manager has to simply define segments and relevant policies and these gets applied across entire network, eliminating complex configurations. Each segment would have its own policies and these polices are carried across the WAN.

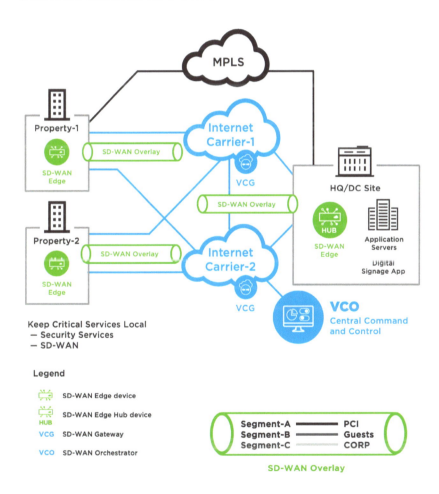

Figure 5.3 Connecting Hospitality Properties with VMware SD-WAN

What You Need to Know

- To compete in a disruptive world, hospitality organizations must deliver a compelling guest experience, gain insight into customers, and maximize efficiency and cost savings.

- Enterprise-grade VMware SD-WAN lets hospitality organizations simplify and streamline network operations with centralized management.

- Dynamic Multi-Path Optimization enhances application performance, aggregating multiple links and steering traffic over the most optimal link available at the time.

- Global segmentation capabilities enable organizations to isolate different types of traffic, such as guest Wi-Fi and PCI traffic, while maintaining business policies and topologies for every segment.

Chapter 6

Bootstrapping Construction Sites with SD-WAN

Business agility and collaboration are top of mind for today's forward-looking construction organizations. In this chapter, we will show how VMware SD-WAN can enable them to build more connected, nimble organizations and extend their market reach.

Requirements: Building Becomes More Collaborative and Agile

Construction business processes are evolving as companies leverage new mobile technologies such as 4G and 5G to connect construction sites with remotely-hosted applications. Firms are increasingly turning to cloud-based solutions to track schedules and manage building supply inventories and project budget and costs. Communication between multiple partners is becoming seamless, as firms increasingly share content with tools that support centralized storage of all project-related files. The Internet has also made remote collaboration common, bringing project managers and on-site teams closer together from any location, for improved efficiency and accountability.

According to Dustin DeVan, CEO of Building Connected, "Before the hammer hits the nail, hundreds and sometimes thousands of businesses communicate with one another to set budgets and decide who's working on what."[12]

Like most industries, construction firms are also under nonstop pressure to make their organizations nimbler so they can turn around projects quickly and move on to the next project. Even a day or two of lost time can drive up costs and bog down progress.

Challenges: Scale and Deliver Applications in the Cloud

To enable the collaboration and agility they need, construction leaders are turning to digital collaboration and the cloud. Cloud technology can dramatically boost efficiencies and productivity, but it requires a dependable, reliable infrastructure.

Establishing a reliable communications infrastructure at remote construction sites is not always easy—especially if telco providers are not available or cannot provide responsive support. Construction firms need the ability to:

- **Set up and configure fast:** Construction sites are often set up in a bare location, with no infrastructure. Firms need a fast, simple way to provision remote sites and connect them to the WAN with the appropriate level of security and corporate compliance. They must safeguard sensitive communications, while providing the performance needed to support rich video collaboration, voice, and other latency-sensitive traffic. Furthermore, they need to establish these new sites without expensive truck rolls and costly on-site IT personnel.

12 "Three Emerging Technologies Impacting the Construction Industry" February 2018, Forbes

- **Maximize compliance:** Policy compliance is essential, especially for construction firms that are collaborating with third-party partners. As they establish their on-site network connections, firms must ensure that firewall and application rules are consistent and in full compliance with company standards—regardless of where they are located. Construction sites do not have onsite network staff, so the equipment stack deployed must be remotely manageable as well as self-healing in the event a network problem occurs. Builders need the ability to rapidly push configurations out to their sites from a single, centralized management station, together with deep visibility to monitor enforcement of policies. Partners expect the access at different construction sites to be identical as well as ubiquitous.

Solution: Faster Deployment, Intelligent Compliance

With a secure, intelligent enterprise-grade VMware SD-WAN, construction firms of all sizes gain the power and flexibility to establish the remote WAN connectivity their teams require to work smoothly together—from any location.

VMware SD-WAN provides rapid deployment for remote construction sites through zero-touch provisioning, fast configuration, and full support for compliance.

Get Onsite Fast with Zero-Touch Deployment

For growing construction organizations that need to set up operations fast, VMware SD-WAN delivers the simplicity and agility they require. Construction employees or administrators on staff can quickly install and provision new sites on their own, with no network team visits or pre-staging needed.

To set up a new job site, an administrator at the construction firm's headquarters creates a configuration and sends an email with an activation key to the installer. An office administrator at the job site can power up the VMware SD-WAN Edge device (Figure 6.1), plug it into the Internet, then click on the activation key to activate and configure the device. Within minutes, employees at the remote site will have access to the Internet and their business-critical cloud or communication applications so they can get productive fast.

VMware SD-WAN can accommodate a variety of broadband links, as well as mobile options such as LTE, providing flexible connectivity options for new construction sites. Construction firms can easily enable their teams in the field to communicate and collaborate with colleagues at their headquarters and other sites—even from sites where no connections existed before. They can start with a dual LTE connection, then add a wired link as soon as it becomes available. Their field office becomes operational as soon as it is loaded off the truck.

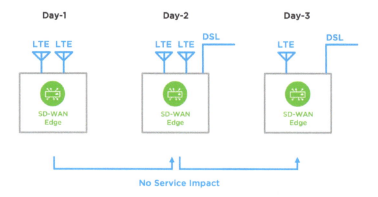

Figure 6.1 Enabling Zero-Touch Provisioning at Construction Sites

Leveraging Profiles to Ensure Compliance

Maintaining compliance and security across a diverse array of remote WAN sites is challenging. Each site may have different requirements in terms of access privileges, security requirements, applications, or other criteria. Furthermore, manually configuring multiple devices to align with profiles is time-consuming and error-prone.

VMware SD-WAN uses the concept of a profile to promote uniform policy use across the network. In contrast to the use of templates, profiles auto-complete settings based on the intent defined in the profile. If a connection to a CASB provider is desired at each of the branches, this only needs to be defined once in the profile. As long as a newly provisioned VMware SD-WAN Edge device is attached to the profile it will be able to access the CASB service. Profiles also allow for local intelligence gathered at the edge to drive a final decision.

VMware SD-WAN simplifies the deployment of services at the branch. One-click service provisioning activates multiple native services and third-party Virtual Network Functions (VNFs) from technology partners at the branch. Using the VMware SD-WAN Orchestrator, construction firms can establish the profiles they need to ensure security and compliance, then push the required configuration to all their sites based on branch role or geographic location (Figure 6.2). Each branch is defined as part of a profile, so firms can apply the policies and configurations they need consistently. Organizations can also apply best-of-breed CASB or VNF services for advanced security.

Figure 6.2 Cloud Security Services

In Focus: Improving Speed, Visibility, and Control in Construction

A major construction firm in Europe was looking for a better way to support customers in remote locations. The organization supported nine branches and more than 1,000 employees, serving large clients in the chemical, energy, food, and steel markets.

The firm operated at customer locations and often had employees working at dozens of sites across Europe. To deliver the speed and agility its clients expected, the firm had to have staff and IT support in place within two days of receiving an order, as well as a fully-functioning WAN connection. If a telco provider could not establish the required connectivity in time, then the firm could use a 4G mobile network as its carrier to support a stable, secure connection.

To extend reliable connectivity quickly and securely, the construction firm chose VMware SD-WAN. This flexible solution made it easy for the firm to choose from a variety of providers and connection protocols to suit specific projects—from MPLS to ADSL and 4G. VMware SD-WAN provided:

- **Increased connection stability:** Dependable connectivity enables employees to communicate and collaborate on projects, regardless of their location. The solution also delivers enhanced speed and a superior user experience, to boost productivity.

- **Full network visibility:** VMware SD-WAN lets network teams manage application traffic and performance more effectively, including as-a-service offerings such as Citrix.

- **Centralized management:** VMware SD-WAN provides complete control over the firm's entire WAN, accelerating tasks like router upgrades at multiple sites to minutes—instead of days or weeks.

The firm looks forward to leveraging VMware SD-WAN for years to come. Scalability is essential in a dynamic industry, and VMware SD-WAN is simple enough for the construction firm to configure and implement on its own. To bring up a new site, the firm can simply deploy a new VMware SD-WAN Edge connect it to the Internet, and the secure connection immediately goes live.

Before and After: The SD-WAN Difference

Before deploying an SD-WAN, construction firms required network staff on-site for new deployments (Figure 6.3).

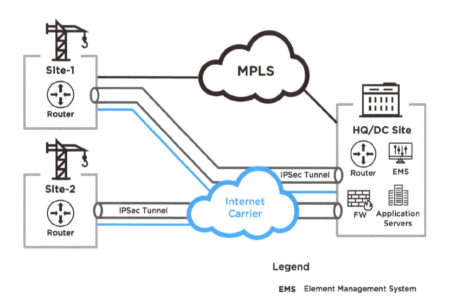

Figure 6.3 Construction Site Before SD-WAN.

With VMware SD-WAN, construction firms can set up a new site in minutes, with no technical staff required to activate it. All links are in active-active mode, and firms can easily aggregate links to download large files.

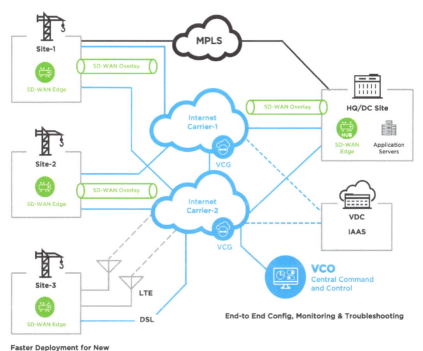

Faster Deployment for New Construction Sites

Figure 6.4 Construction Site with VMware SD-WAN

What You Need to Know

- Enterprise-grade VMware SD-WAN lets construction firms rapidly deploy and configure remote sites to support collaboration and cloud-based applications.

- To help maximize compliance, VMware SD-WAN enables policy-based provisioning to multiple sites without costly manual configuration and management.

- VMware SD-WAN is fast and easy for construction firms to deploy on their own, without expensive help from network teams.

- VMware SD-WAN enables construction firms to rapidly scale and extend the infrastructure as needs change, to boost agility and meet future business imperatives.

Chapter 7

Unleashing the Potential of IoT

Digital transformation is driving changes across every industry, and the IoT is playing a key role. Smart, connected devices and low-power sensors provide real-time data to give organizations better insight and control.

In this chapter, we will discuss how SD-WAN enables today's increasingly connected organizations to unlock the potential of the Internet of Things (IoT).

Requirements: Enabling More Connections in More Environments

IoT is taking shape rapidly driven by data, mobility, and a proliferation of new devices. As an example, energy companies are tracking power usage in real-time and building smarter grids with connected metering systems .

Healthcare providers are tracking patient condition in real-time from anywhere. Smart vehicles are emerging that will transport passengers without requiring human drivers. Self-healing machines on assembly lines are empowering the supply chain. According to a survey by IHS Markit, there are 20 billion connected devices globally as of 2017[13]. And the trend is gaining momentum.

Although IoT adoption continues to grow and evolve, firms will still face many of the same issues that they do with other network solutions such as cloud, as-a-service, and collaboration technologies. As the volume of devices, connections, and data on their environments multiplies, their infrastructures will become more complex. Running multiple cloud and on-premises environments increases fragmentation and introduces security, management, and compliance concerns. Manufacturing and Industrial Internet of Things (IIoT) environments also have specific challenges and priorities which we will explore in this chapter.

SD-WAN technology can play a key role in helping organizations mitigate complexity, ensure compliance, and effectively manage and scale their IoT infrastructure.

Challenges: Enabling and Scaling IoT

One of the fundamental challenges for IoT infrastructures is the scale of deployments. The number of devices connected to the IoT is forecast to be 75.4 billion by 2025, up from 15.4 billion devices in 2015[14]—with an accompanying flood of data.

---

13 "IoT Trend Watch 2017," IHS Markit
14 "IoT Platforms: Enabling the Internet of Things," HIS Markit, 2016.

The sheer size and complexity of IoT applications creates real challenges for network teams:

Cloud optimization: Data is the fuel that powers IoT, and cloud-based applications are critical to enabling organizations to its unlock potential. On the IoT, cloud-based applications enable organizations to collect, interpret, and transmit data via connected sensors and things. Applications and systems need a cloud-optimized solution to connect to the data they need, regardless of location.

Traffic prioritization: IoT applications are often time-sensitive. Medical sensors, transportation applications, and industrial processes all produce a stream of data that must be prioritized, managed, and aggregated in real-time. Rich media traffic requires an overlay process to manage latency and jitter across a variety of networks. Aggregation of data often takes place at a remote location where compute power is more readily available.

Security and compliance: As organizations grow and become more fragmented and the complexity of an environment increases, network security challenges multiply, too. The more connected devices and low-power sensors there are in an IoT environment, the more potential for security breaches. Securing a diverse array of remote WAN sites is not easy, and each site might have specific requirements based on applications, location, or other aspects. Organizations need a consistent, automated way to establish profiles needed for security and compliance. Then they can push the required configuration to all their sites based on branch role or geographic location.

Special IoT Challenges for IIoT and Manufacturers

Manufacturing is a particularly promising arena for IoT applications, and a key driver of economies. In 2016, manufacturing accounted for 11.7 percent of GDP in the U.S. economy according to the Bureau of Economic Analysis[15]. Through initiatives like Industry 4.0, manufacturers are seeking better ways to monitor physical processes and make faster, better decisions utilizing a smart factory[16]. The initiative is based on enabling devices to communicate and cooperate with each other and with humans in real-time both internally and across the value chain.

---

15 http://www.nam.org/Newsroom/Top-20-Facts-About-Manufacturing/
16 "What Everyone Must Know About Industry 4.0," Bernard Marr, Forbes, June 20, 2016

Manufacturers are also embracing new technologies such as:

- Artificial intelligence (AI)
- Augmented reality (AR)
- Robotics
- 3D printing

Manufacturers adopting IIoT solutions face distinct challenges as they seek to connect devices at remote sites and factories across geographically dispersed locations.

Network segmentation support: A key requirement for manufacturing WANs is the simplification of network design and security—especially network segmentation. Manufacturers frequently segment networks as a way of separating and isolating individual product lines into sub-networks to deliver enhanced security and improve performance. Manufacturing networks are part of a complex, interconnected value chain of suppliers, partners, and third parties. If one of these parties is compromised, then the security threat could spread through data sharing across the extended enterprise.

Solution: Unleashing the Potential of IoT Across Industries

VMware SD-WAN is ready and capable of stepping into the role of managing IoT with an inherent ability to support IoT initiatives. It enables organizations to address their IoT implementation challenges by applying a software-defined networking (SDN) approach that brings together all of their devices, sensors, and dispersed environments under a common, fully manageable solution.

VMware SD-WAN has built-in IoT support that comes in the form of commodity traffic offload to inexpensive transport options, with segmentation and security. Enabling rapid deployment, a business policy approach, and deep insight and control into the extended enterprise, VMware SD-WAN positions manufacturers and other organizations to realize the full benefits of advanced IoT deployments. When paired with a partner solution, such as an offering from the VMware IoT partner ecosystem, VMware SD-WAN forms a powerful foundation to build on.

Simple Cloud Deployment

The three-tier IoT architecture of sensors, gateways, and the cloud is an excellent fit for an SD-WAN framework. With VMware SD-WAN, each sensor corresponds to an endpoint, while the IoT Gateway interoperates with the VMware SD-WAN Edge. Organizations can choose from a variety of IoT cloud services as well as IIoT offerings. These cloud services can be inserted or chained into the SD-WAN framework, dramatically simplifying the setup and deployment of an IoT network.

In a hybrid network, VMware SD-WAN lets enterprises route traffic through the best choice of WAN path based on an application's requirements for network security, QoS, and other criteria. VMware SD-WAN lets enterprises take advantage of the benefits of IoT, while offloading IoT traffic – which is typically well-suited to low-cost broadband – directly to the Internet, instead of using the more expensive private core. VMware SD-WAN enables an extremely flexible solution that lets network administrators easily reconfigure the network to align with their needs.

Powering Traffic Prioritization

VMware SD-WAN enables organizations to ensure high performance for latency-sensitive traffic, to ensure not only smooth performance but also close coordination between interdependent IoT processes. Network teams and administrators can customize and create their own unique policies to govern a network's traffic using VMware SD-WAN. The solution provides the control required to prioritize traffic ensuring that high priority packets can pass over most efficient network paths for their specific type of traffic.

Using VMware SD-WAN Dynamic Multipath Optimization technology, an organization can aggregate broadband Internet, 4G-LTE, and MPLS circuits with application-aware, per-packet link steering, and on-demand remediation. The result is maximum performance over any transport. VMware SD-WAN also provides consolidated monitoring and visibility across multiple WAN links and service providers both of which simplify management.

Ensuring Security and Simplifying Deployment

The VMware SD-WAN solution simplifies the deployment of services at the branch. One-click service provisioning activates multiple VMware SD-WAN native services and third-party virtual network functions from technology partners on the branch Edge. Using the VMware SD-WAN Orchestrator, manufacturers and other firms can establish the profiles they need to ensure security and compliance, and then push the required configuration to all their sites based on branch role or geographic location. Each branch is part of a profile.

VMware SD-WAN Meets Specific Needs of IIoT and Manufacturers

For manufacturers, SD-WANs can deliver the agility, availability, and trust required for advanced IIoT manufacturing applications.

- 61 percent of manufacturers expect to achieve WAN optimization from their SD-WAN.[17]

- 67 percent plan to use SD-WAN in the next 1-2 years.[18]

In Focus: Applying Next-Generation Industrial Automation Principles to Network Innovation

A major communications service provider based in the European Union was seeking to make its operations more secure, efficient, and economical by implementing an Industry 4.0 smart factory initiative. It was exploring a variety of technologies, including IoT, cybersecurity, big data analytics, augmented reality, robotics, and several other initiatives.

The provider had already deployed an SDN-based data center networking framework to enable its operators to bring remote sites online more rapidly. To set the stage for new efficiencies, its engineers had begun to explore how next-generation industrial automation and network architectures could further build on its framework.

Scalability was a top concern for the provider. The organization wanted to test whether its SDN and data center framework would could be extended to international sites while continuing to offer the same level of visibility, agility, and management capabilities available on its smaller networks. Working closely with its industrial partner, the provider developed a prototype network that would connect the robotics and 3D printing command center at its headquarters with other robots in other countries. The firm would need to accomplish the initiative with minimal disruption and no redesigns to its existing network. The initiative would also need to automate orchestration of all the various components needed for 3D printing and ensure reliable connectivity and uptime. The firm was also seeking to support link aggregation, and the ability to transfer large data models to the printer in a shorter period of time, for faster output.

---

17 SD-WAN Enabling Digital Transformation in Manufacturing, IDC infographic sponsored by Comcast, March, 2018
18 SD-WAN Enabling Digital Transformation in Manufacturing, IDC infographic sponsored by Comcast, March, 2018

To enable its IIoT initiative, the service provider augmented its existing network using the VMware SD-WAN solution as an overlay to connect and enable its end devices.

The solution provided:

- Consolidated monitoring and visibility across multiple WAN links and service providers to reduce complexity, simplify management, and minimize outages.

- High performance for robotic commands utilizing VMware SD-WAN Dynamic Multipath Optimization technology for application-aware control.

- The ability to add network services at the edge, in the cloud, or in a datacenter through business policies which handle optimal gateway selection, distributed QoS configurations, automatic VPN connections, and other tasks.

- Rapid, plug-and-play setup and connectivity.

The new solution enables the service provider to scale IIoT applications leveraging SDN capabilities across sites even thousands of miles away and scales easily to deliver resilient, real-time, secure networking whenever and wherever it is needed. It lets the provider scale its printing processes to 3D, providing remote printing components near the users that need them most, eliminating the need for shipping and maintaining inventory.

Before and After: The SD-WAN Difference

As IoT deployments become more pervasive at industrial sites, data generated by sensors and actuators is transported over the existing network infrastructure that is available at the factory (Figure 7.1). These organizations commonly utilize one or more private network connections to access applications hosted in a centralized data center.

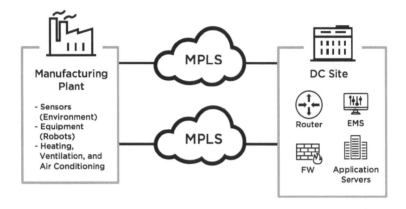

Legend

EMS   Element Management System

FW   Firewall

Figure 7.1 IoT Before SD-WAN.

When VMware SD-WAN is deployed to the factory floor, sensor data that is generated can be transmitted in real time to a centralized datacenter or cloud collector that offers analytics services (Figure 7.2). Organizations can easily prioritize critical traffic flows that are time sensitive on the network, while taking advantage of an increased mix of network providers and access technologies to reduce the risk of single-point-of-failure that can impact telemetry data.

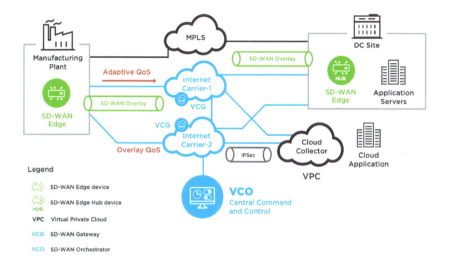

Figure 7.2 Enabling IoT Deployments with VMware SD-WAN

What You Need to Know

- For IoT applications across a variety of industries, VMware SD-WAN provides scalability, easy deployment, and centralized management required to support vast arrays of connected devices and their data.

- VMware SD-WAN lets organizations prioritize traffic to ensure high priority packets are allowed to pass across the most efficient network paths.

- Organizations can establish the profiles required for security and compliance, then push the required configuration to all their sites, based on branch role or geographic location.

- Cloud services can be inserted or chained into the VMware SD-WAN framework making the task of setting up an IoT network simple.

- For manufacturers, VMware SD-WAN enables IIoT applications by providing support for highly available networks required for extended supply chains as well as sophisticated network segmentation and security.

Chapter 8

Cloud Readiness for Evolving Enterprise Needs

VMware SD-WAN can deliver measurable benefits to organizations of all sizes. In this chapter, we will focus on how it can address requirements for enterprises spanning the spectrum from small and mid-sized to large, multinational organizations. We will explore the common challenges companies face in terms of flexible and secure deployment, together with the need for high performance and the ability to scale to multiple branch sites.

Requirements: Delivering Scalable, Manageable Access Across the WAN and Cloud

Technology is leveling the playing field for the enterprise. With the right network infrastructure and IT strategy, organizations can be more competitive and differentiate their themselves more effectively in their industry.

Enterprise infrastructures often consist of multiple data center environments, including on-premises and legacy data centers with a variety of third-party network devices. Beyond the data center, organizations must provide smooth, seamless access to all their WAN sites, including those connected via Internet links.

For enterprises of all sizes, operational simplicity is critical for its IT solutions. According to James A. Browning, vice president and distinguished analyst at Gartner, when all factors are equal, CIOs should choose the solution that leads in operational effectiveness and has the lowest total cost of ownership.[19]

Although organizations vary greatly in size and scope, they share a wide variety of common needs. Enterprises require:

- Network agility
- Ease of deployment
- Centralized management and control
- Lower TCO (Total Cost of Ownership)

Let's discuss each of these requirements one by one, then explore how VMware SD-WAN enables enterprises to address them.

Network Agility

To keep pace in a fast-paced world of digital transformation, network teams need to support their business stakeholders by providing fast access to the applications and technologies they need—as soon as they are needed.

Ensuring Access to Applications Anytime, Anywhere

Today's increasingly mobile employees work from a variety of locations—in the office, at home, on the move, and at customer sites. They access the needed applications from many different devices, and increasingly these applications are cloud-based.

19 https://www.gartner.com/smarterwithgartner/4-trends-that-impact-how-midsize-enterprises-deal-with-it-vendors/

Whether they are utilizing a human resources site or a Customer Relationship Management (CRM) application from the desktop or a sales tool on a tablet, these employees need consistent, high-performance access to their most critical applications, both on-premises in the data center, as well as in the cloud. It's up to network teams to ensure that access—however, whenever, and wherever employees are working from. Delivering ubiquitous access, together with the right level of performance and security, is not easy on a traditional infrastructure with disparate management tools and limited control and visibility.

Building a Better On-Ramp to Cloud

Applications are moving from an on-premises deployment model to a cloud model. However, enterprises typically backhaul cloud traffic through their data center sites over private links.

MPLS is a private network architecture and is designed for any-to-any connectivity of enterprise locations. As applications migrate to cloud services and private cloud facilities, a managed Internet breakout from the MPLS creates undesirable backhaul conditions that introduce unwanted latency and jitter. Organizations seek a different approach that lets them break traffic out to cloud destinations, directly from the branch location over Internet links, and augment the existing MPLS deployments. This allows for high quality interconnects to other locations and datacenters over the MPLS link—while at the same time providing reliable connections to business-critical SaaS applications without adding excessive latency.

An MPLS architecture cannot always deliver the dexterity and agility required by traffic flowing to a frequently-changing variety of "off-network" destinations such as cloud-based sites. The constraints and costs require substantial lead time for planning and deployment.

Since MPLS is built to support private connections, enterprises need to shift bandwidth to Dedicated Internet Access (DIA) or a broadband link. However, neither of these circuits include performance guarantees (SLAs) that are common on MPLS circuits. This forces enterprises to depend on circuits that may not provide the performance required to support their business-critical applications. At the same time, SaaS offerings do not have an SLA expectation that can be supported by public links.

Support DevOps for Agility

Many organizations are transforming existing network management groups into more agile DevOps teams that use APIs to integrate solutions into business workflows and processes. The use of ReST APIs enables organizations to reach deeper into solutions and modify and monitor objects at a finer granularity than ever before. Information elements can be dynamically integrated into existing business applications to bring data together for a higher degree of visibility and correlation.

APIs also enable organizations to interface multiple vendor solutions, without requiring extensive reprogramming and customization for formal integration.

Support Mergers and Acquisitions

Most enterprises are constantly growing and expanding, and many are going through mergers and acquisitions. To ensure that these bold moves are successful, network administrators require a strategy and platform that enables them to rapidly integrate networks from acquired companies, provide transition plans, and incorporate their operations seamlessly into the global WAN.

Ease of Deployment

Today's enterprises have more choices available to them, but they need to pick a solution that gives them the freedom to take advantage of deployment options that best suit their business, whether cloud- or software-based, hardware based, or a hybrid.

Rapidly Provision and Optimize New Sites

Network teams are assuming more strategic tasks, increasingly focusing less on "keeping the lights on," and more on driving business growth. As roles change, CIOs are finding it increasingly difficult to balance these needs and are looking for ways to utilize their resources more effectively.

Speeding deployment of new branch sites is an attractive target. Network teams may spend a great deal of their time configuring individual branch sites. Each site requires a unique topology with unique configuration and link types.

Broadband circuits offer several advantages for setting up new sites. They are more easily available and can typically be provisioned very quickly, and augment MPLS links. evolve, and capacity issues emerge, it's often easier to add extra bandwidth via LTE or other broadband options to pick up the slack.

When it comes to management and configuration, IT professionals should not have to waste time manually defining rules for thousands of applications and links. Furthermore, adjusting QoS policies based on available bandwidth is simply not possible with most legacy WAN solutions. Network teams need a solution that lets them abstract the business policy from the underlying transport. The system should dynamically pick the best link for the application.

Connecting Data Centers and Non-SD-WAN Sites

Most enterprises have gradually piled up many different network environments and platforms over the years. Connecting these legacy datacenter sites, which may have a mix of third-party devices, to branch sites on the company WAN is difficult. Network teams needs a better way to continue to get value out of its existing technology investments. New branch sites must be able to join the WAN automatically, via secure VPN, and enjoy access to the same resources that are available at other branch locations. These sites also require access to enterprise data centers that do not reside on the SD-WAN, and cloud-data centers.

Network teams are constantly modifying and scaling the network infrastructure to address changing business needs and new business imperatives. In some cases, an enterprise might begin migrating to VMware SD-WAN in phases. Perhaps some of its branch sites will have already transitioned to the new architecture, but its existing data center maintains a traditional architecture. How can an enterprise connect its branch sites to a legacy data center environment, smoothly and dependably?

Smarter ISP Choices

As enterprises extend their infrastructures on a global basis, it becomes difficult to find a single provider that can deliver networking services in all locations that the enterprise operates from. Although a preferred global provider may be chosen, this provider must often rely on regional carriers to deliver the local loop circuit to the branch location. This selection of the regional carrier is based on partnerships that are in place to achieve global network coverage, but it also inherently restricts choice and promotes carrier lock-in. Introducing the flexibility to use any regional carrier and independence from established carrier partnerships can decrease circuit provisioning lead times, and potentially reduce costs.

By adding more than one carrier into the branch networking bandwidth mix, enterprises reduce the risk of being impacted by a single carrier degradation and create a more robust WAN link blend.

Opening carrier choice will also enable diverse access technologies to be deployed, further minimizing the risk of impact on the branch in the event of a carrier infrastructure problem. For example, a network administrator may wish to leverage new technologies such as 5G on an ad-hoc basis as they become available in the region. It minimizes exposure to the effects of environmental (such as weather in the case of 4G) and architectural (eg shared medium in the case of cable) factors on a single access technology.

Centralized Management and Control

Diverse enterprise environments that reside in a variety of different locations and platforms present real management challenges. These enterprises need a centralized way to gain visibility, insight, and control across the infrastructure, for effective management, security, and compliance.

Traditional Element Management (EMS) systems are focused on device inventory and providing isolated configuration changes limited to a single device. Network-wide changes are difficult to deploy with EMS systems. This increases the time needed to make essential configuration changes.

Taking Control of Unsanctioned Applications

People have more application choices than ever, but they don't always coordinate with their network teams when utilizing them. Individual teams or users may take the initiative to employ their own, unsanctioned applications on the WAN, to accomplish specific business goals fast—but are not under the control of network teams.

For example, a small business team might establish a box.com account to collaborate with partners and exchange files—even though network teams may have previously standardized on Microsoft OneDrive. Although box.com meets short-term business needs, employing two separate file sharing platforms can lead to data leaking as one of the applications is not set up according to business policy guidelines. Gaining visibility into which applications are used on the network is essential for network teams seeking to optimize management and compliance. Policies to block such applications can be rolled out with ease.

To regain control and ensure the best possible health and performance across their networks, network teams need insight into how much of its WAN bandwidth is being used by unsanctioned applications. They require visibility into the type of traffic utilized by its WAN circuits, an understanding of how their enterprise is prioritizing traffic, and whether it is allowing these unsanctioned applications to failover to MPLS in the event an Internet link goes down. Network teams also need more effective tools and techniques to help them identify these unsanctioned applications.

Understanding Data Center Traffic

Infrastructure environments are becoming more diverse. To scale their capabilities and modernize their applications more quickly, organizations have turned to public and private clouds. In a recent survey of cloud users, 93.6 percent of organizations indicated that they would utilize multiple types of cloud deployment options within 12 months—up from 85.2 percent.[20]

As time passes and cloud computing matures, many are finding that their organizations have accumulated multiple public cloud services, along with an on-premises data center.

To manage and optimize performance on these diverse environments, network teams need to understand which destinations traffic is flowing to. For example, they need visibility and trending information on the volume of traffic destined for SaaS services, compared to on-premises and hosted applications in the data center. Network teams also require insight into usage patterns, including which groups and individuals are using which applications—and how much. This will allow for bandwidth planning as more users onboard in existing or new locations on the corporate network.

Safeguarding Sensitive Data

Security is top of mind for organizations of every size. Diverse, decentralized cloud-based environments can create security concerns, because consistently enforcing security policies is difficult. Enterprise organizations need a way to apply security across the cloud and their network, while minimizing complexity at branch offices.

In the diverse enterprise world, security requirements vary depending on application, user, device, and many other criteria. To apply the appropriate level of security across diverse devices and environments, network teams require stateful, context-aware next-generation firewall protection, which can provide control over micro-applications, as well support for protocol-hopping applications like Skype and other peer-to-peer applications. The solution should be user, device, and OS-aware, and enable organizations to accurately classify traffic flows to apply business policies that ensure these are in a protected performance envelope and meet regulatory requirements.

Scaling for Growth

As organizations grow and expand a global office footprint, a key concern is how the WAN network can be expanded to support multiple thousands of locations—each monitored according to corporate policy and subject to business policies that have been established.

From time to time, enterprise organizations experience not just steady growth, but explosive growth. In rapid growth situations, maintaining visibility and insight into the state of the network under a high rate of change is even more essential.

20 "IDC CloudView," IDC, April, 2017

Capacity Planning from Link Point of View

As network teams assume a more strategic role in driving business growth, capacity planning has become more important. IT professionals need accurate insight into how much bandwidth is used, and the flexibility to add circuits on demand without the need to make policy changes. Instead of modifying a policy, they can simply apply a policy to the new bandwidth. Legacy networking solutions require manual balancing of load to a new circuit. This manual approach is problematic if the conditions of that circuit change.

Cost Reduction

Like any business, enterprises are under constant pressure to do more with less. They need a solution that can help them control costs, while gaining the full value from their technology investments.

Improving Cost Control

As enterprises expand, they are constantly seeking better ways to control the cost of extending their network to branch sites. Consider the average cost of supporting a branch site. An MPLS connection is likely more expensive than a Dedicated Internet Access (DIA) connection, which in turn is more expensive compared to broadband Internet connections. Furthermore, MPLS and DIA links are often placed in standby mode and are treated as an insurance policy. This is not a cost-effective approach to ensure network availability, and delivering the circuit takes time. Given the difference in cost between broadband and MPLS lines, it's not surprising that many enterprises are augmenting their MPLS with a broader choice of lower-cost public links.

Why is the cost of implementation so much lower with broadband circuits, compared to DIA? Broadband requires less equipment to connect links and is based on standardized Ethernet handoffs. Broadband links are also generally more available and require less planning to implement. They can also be more easily replaced in the event the provider circuit does not meet performance expectations.

Although broadband links are available at a lower cost, their quality can be compromised. Broadband Internet may experience congestion, creating increased latency, packet loss, and jitter. To overcome these challenges, organizations need a cost-effective solution that lets them extend secure and high-quality communication to all their branches via multiple WAN connections.

Reducing Dependency on Global Private Core Networks (MPLS)

Minimizing interdependencies is another top IT challenge. As cloud services adoption accelerates, enterprises are moving their applications out of existing data centers into the cloud. Cloud applications create interdependencies just as on-premises applications do, but they do not require the bandwidth of a global private enterprise core. Many network administrators are observing a decreased use of their global core infrastructures—and a decreased need to continue to operate it the same way.

Since the global private core is a large cost center, enterprises are constantly seeking ways to minimize use and make operations more efficient. MPLS cost is a function of bandwidth, distance between locations, and the number of connected locations. Network teams are seeking solutions that can utilize regional hubs for connectivity, as well as reduce the number of locations they are connecting.

Solution: Enabling WAN Access Everywhere, Aligned to Enterprise Imperatives

VMware SD-WAN lets enterprises address the challenges that today's multi-cloud, on-premise diverse organizations face. Through a software-defined approach, it delivers enterprise-grade application performance to users at every location, on any device. Let's explore how VMware SD-WAN helps organizations address the four key challenges listed above.

Powering Network Agility

VMware SD-WAN is cloud-delivered, and software based, to power the business agility enterprises need. It lets enterprises rapidly adapt to changing needs, including adding access to cloud-based services, standing up new branches or remote offices, and dynamic routing of all traffic, for optimized application and data delivery.

Access to Applications Anywhere, Anytime

VMware SD-WAN enables organizations to establish smooth access to applications from anywhere, whether on premises or in the cloud. It employs a software-defined approach where each networking function is virtualized and delivered as a service. Enterprises can take advantage of dependable network connectivity, application access, performance, and security, regardless of location.

VMware SD-WAN delivers this connectivity regardless of transport type. It automatically detects the type of link employed in the WAN, as well as bandwidth, packet loss, latency and jitter. Applications are instantly identified, and their traffic is steered in the most efficient way, based on centrally-controlled business and security policies.

For enterprises that need access to applications in the cloud, VMware SD-WAN Gateways provide an optimized cloud on-ramp to the doorstep of software-as-a-service (SaaS) and infrastructure-as-a-service (IaaS) offerings (Figure 8.1)

1) Non-critical traffic utilizes the underlay, offloading low-priority traffic from the corporate network at the earliest point and freeing up resources for business applications.

2) Enterprises can ensure performance of Internet and SaaS traffic by directing it to an available VMware SD-WAN Gateway using the SD-WAN overlay. Should the security posture demand it, the traffic can be forwarded from the VMware SD-WAN Gateway to an IPSec-attached CASB service for further inspection, before it is released towards its final SaaS destination.

3) A secure tunnel from the VMware SD-WAN Gateway enables connectivity to an IaaS cloud. Branches connect to the VMware SD-WAN Gateway using an VMware SD-WAN overlay tunnel after which the traffic is sent from the VMware SD-WAN Gateway to the IaaS provider via secure tunnel.

4) For on-premises applications and Internet backhaul, the enterprise connects its branch site to the data center over the VMware SD-WAN secured overlay tunnel. This can be used for Internet backhauling should user traffic need processing from a centralized firewall hosted in the corporate datacenter site. For example, an organization might wish to use this approach to support a centralized firewall, rather than CASB, to inspect Internet-bound traffic.

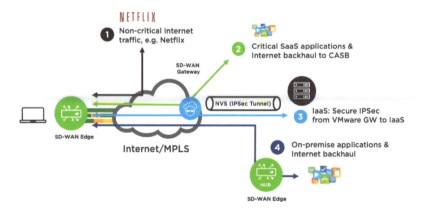

Figure 8.1 Accessing Applications Anywhere, Anytime

VMware SD-WAN Gateways are fully automated, managed and operated by VMware SD-WAN, for plug-and-play connectivity. They can also be hosted in the cloud and managed and operated by service provider partners. Organizations may also choose to host gateways in an enterprise regional hub.

VMware SD-WAN Gateway

This cloud network is:

- **Multi-tenant and worldwide:** A distributed network of multi-tenant gateways lets organizations achieve the best possible connectivity to cloud services.

- **Secure and compliant:** To help organizations meet corporate and regulatory requirements, VMware SD-WAN Gateways reside in datacenters with robust Tier IV SSAE 16 Type II security. For additional protection, organizations can easily provision end-to-end cloud VPN and security services, such as firewall, and web security from VMware SD-WAN by VeloCloud and its partners.

- **Scalable and dependable:** With VMware SD-WAN, enterprises can automatically orchestrate scalable, redundant gateway capacity when and where needed. These services can support enterprise grade branch-to-branch, branch-to-datacenter, and branch-to-cloud access, while eliminating backhauls and unreliable, "best effort" paths.

Enabling Nimble DevOps Teams

VMware SD-WAN provides an excellent platform that lets organizations set the stage for better agility through DevOps. Organizations can build custom portals to extend distributed information in a cohesive fashion to executives or administrators. If access to the Orchestrator is not desirable for a broader audience, select components, such as public IP addresses and providers of the links attached to a branch, can be extracted using the ReST API, and incorporated into an existing management application.

DevOps can also be used to rapidly deploy specialized features needed by the enterprise. For example, a company might wish to establish a time-based policy to optimize data backup, where backup traffic is prioritized over user traffic after business hours.

Ease of Deployment

VMware SD-WAN gives organizations the freedom of choice they need to employ any deployment option, whether cloud, software, or hardware-based—including their existing legacy equipment.

Connecting and Scaling Legacy Data Centers

For organizations seeking to maintain connectivity to their existing legacy data centers, VMware SD-WAN provides a scalable approach to growth.

Organizations can apply VMware SD-WAN as an overlay to their existing network, gaining the agility capabilities and support for new branches, without requiring new configuration of the legacy infrastructure. There's no need to manually reconfigure existing equipment like routers and switches in the data center or send staff to individual branch sites for management tasks. Instead, organizations can continue to use the branch connectivity they prefer, whether it's broadband or leased lines. They can set up new VMware SD-WAN branch site configurations automatically, from a central orchestrator. And they can move traffic over self-configuring VPN tunnels to an VMware SD-WAN gateway, which can reside at an on-site data center or at any cloud location.

VMware SD-WAN also enables seamless connectivity with legacy data centers that include third-party devices. Organizations can rapidly establish a secure VPN tunnel from an VMware SD-WAN gateway to any third-party device that resides at the data center. This eliminates the need for each site to be individually configured with a tunnel to access a legacy site. Instead, the VPN tunneling from VMware SD-WAN Gateway to a non-SD-WAN site is centrally provisioned through the VMware SD-WAN Orchestrator (Figure 8.2). This capability is especially valuable for organizations with multiple data centers that have only partially migrated select sites to SD-WAN. The approach also enables redundancy, for improved service availability if a link should experience issues or failure.

The VMware SD-WAN Gateway will initiate a secure tunnel to the non-SD-WAN sites shown in FIgure 8.2. There is no need for branch sites to build individual IPSec tunnels to these sites, and profiles enable configurations to be applied with a single click.

For example, an organization could deliver a cloud VPN configuration to 50 branch sites that are part of the "Corporate Branches" profile. This means that each branch site will have an overlay between the branch edge device to the VMware SD-WAN Gateway. From VMware SD-WAN Gateway, traffic will be sent over the secure VPN tunnel.

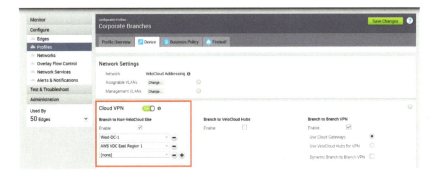

Figure 8.2 VMware SD-WAN Orchestrator Cloud VPN for Non-SD-WAN Sites

Improving Access to Global Private Core Networks

Organizations can choose a hub site to provide access to the global MPLS core network. However, since the private global network no longer needs to be extended to each and every branch, they can constrain its use to interconnect to the private core only at selected regional hub sites. Regional hub sites are commonly larger branch offices that already host additional applications to support the consumer base in the region. They often have more diverse network connections, including access circuits to the private global core network.

VMware SD-WAN functions as a last mile optimization technology, enabling organizations to utilize a set of regional carriers to construct a VMware SD-WAN overlay service.

Centralized Management and Control

To provide the centralized control, robust security and compliance that enterprises need, VMware SD-WAN employs a centrally-located orchestrator. This orchestrator is a multi-tenant, virtual machine deployed in the cloud or on-premises. The VMware SD-WAN Orchestrator provides centralized enterprise-wide installation, configuration, and real-time monitoring, in addition to orchestrating the data flow through the cloud network (Figure 8.3). It also monitors all network activity, problem alerts, and remote remediation of issues.

The VeloCloud Orchestrator provides access to device and link status of globally-deployed edges at a single glance. Alarms can be set to actively notify administrators of unexpected activity that may impact the user experience at the branch.

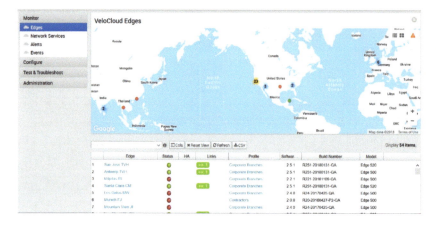

Figure 8.3 VMware SD-WAN Orchestrator Monitor UI Showing
Map and List View for Sites

Policy-Based Provisioning and Control

Prioritizing latency-sensitive traffic is always challenging, especially
when extended across geographically dispersed locations of an
enterprise. The challenges multiply when organizations want to bring
up new branch offices at new sites.

VMware SD-WAN lets organizations enable prioritization at the
business level, by simply stating business policies. VMware SD-WAN
business policy hides the underlying complexity of configuring
complex rules (Figure 8.4). Administrators can set a policy to constrain
an application to any public wired link, without needing to manually
configure individual ports per branch site.

In this example, transport groups allow administrators to convey an
intent to restrict traffic from using only public wired links for a specific
application. With a traditional solution flows would have to be mapped
to a physical port, which can vary per site. With VMware SD-WAN, this
determination is made each time a new link is connected to the VMware
SD-WAN Edge device to support intent-based policies.

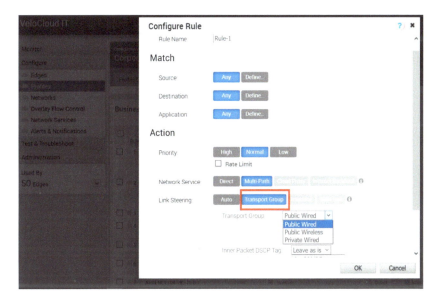

Figure 8.4 VMware SD-WAN Orchestrator Showing Simplified
Business Policy Using Transport Group

VMware SD-WAN supports both centralized policy management as
well as distributed policy enforcement. The VMware SD-WAN
Orchestrator provides the policy that is enacted at the edge, based on
real-time measurements it obtains from the attached transport links.

This policy-based approach is a powerful technique to drive queuing
and bandwidth allocation, as well as path steering and on-demand
remediation techniques. VMware SD-WAN provides these features
without the complex configuration tasks required for traditional WAN
environments. Automated path steering helps optimize performance,
and organizations may also choose to use business policies to specify
specific link usage for compliance or security. For example, an
organization may wish to choose a "Mandatory" option to constrain an
application to a specific path, such as private wired links for PCI traffic
(Figure 8.5). Even if the overlay goes down, that application's traffic
will not pass through a public link.

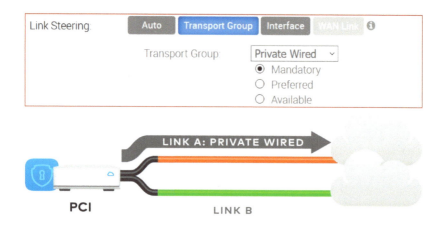

Figure 8.5 VMware SD-WAN Orchestrator Business
Policy UI with Link Steering Options

Ensuring Security and Compliance

To provide protection in a fast-changing threat landscape, VMware
SD-WAN offers a flexible choice of architectures that enable
organizations to build a solution that best aligns with their
security needs.

VMware SD-WAN provides the all-in-one management that is especially
important for organizations with limited IT resources. It provides a single
management station that can reside in the cloud or on-premises,
providing visibility and control across the organization's environments,
including data center use and SaaS applications. This single, uniform
point of control enables network teams to enforce policies consistently,
while providing the tools and insight needed to configure, monitor and
troubleshoot the entire SD-WAN network. These business policies can
provide a hierarchical framework that lets network teams ensure that
security is correctly and consistently applied, while also enabling the
flexibility to override policies when needed.

The solution also lets network teams insert local, third-party, and cloud
security services wherever and whenever they are needed. It supports
cloud access security brokers (CASBs) for smooth integration with
leading security solutions from best-of-bread partners. The VMware
SD-WAN Orchestrator enables one-click provisioning of virtual
services in the branch, the cloud, or the enterprise datacenter
(Figure 8.6).

Some examples of these distributed services include:

1) Security service insertion at branch site, such as Palo Alto Security VNF.

2) Direct IPSec connection (non-SD-WAN overlay) from a branch site to cloud security providers.

3) Cloud security services accessed through the VMware SD-WAN Gateways, enabling branch sites to leverage VMware SD-WAN Dynamic Multi-Path Optimization, with no configuration required on the edge devices. Traffic from the branch site to the VMware SD-WAN gateway is on VMware SD-WAN overlay.

4) Next-generation firewall services in the datacenter, with Internet and SaaS traffic backhauled to the datacenter firewall.

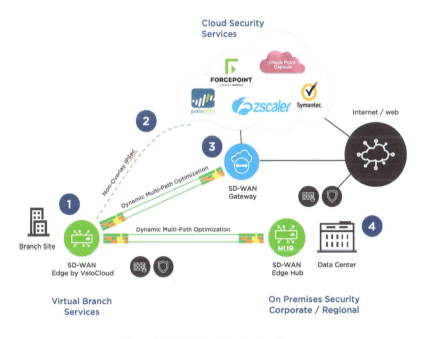

Figure 8.6 Distributed Service Insertion

Enabling Capacity Planning and Controlling Unsanctioned Applications

Network teams are constantly evaluating bandwidth needs, both for short-term initiatives as well as long-term strategic planning. For example, an organization running Microsoft Office 365 may be considering adding more bandwidth to its cloud data center to support escalating traffic.

VMware SD-WAN makes adding bandwidth a zero-downtime event. Once the link is connected to an available port, the VMware SD-WAN Edge will characterize the bandwidth. After that step is complete, it will be added to the bandwidth blend, and is ready to be consumed.

Gaining actionable insight into link utilization is critical to making decisions to augment link capacity or to deprioritize non-business critical applications in favor of business-critical and relevant applications. VMware SD-WAN provides the centralized management and insight needed for better, faster strategic decisions.

The VMware SD-WAN Orchestrator provides richer and deep analytics on the WAN links and application side. It provides the visibility and insight organizations need to better understand and control their applications and infrastructure, and make more informed decisions about how to best optimize it.

This component of the VMware SD-WAN provides support for centralized installation, configuration and real time monitoring—across the enterprise organization. It not only provides support for on-premises traffic but orchestrates data flows through the cloud network.

The VMware SD-WAN controllers collect and distribute enterprise-wide routing information to the rest of the SD-WAN network and allow the Orchestrator to centrally visualize this information for easy inspection and troubleshooting, rather than performing these actions on individual networking elements. VMware SD-WAN utilizes a centralized routing table called an Overlay Flow Control (OFC) table (Figure 8.7). The OFC shows all learned and detected attached networks with the egress nodes on the SD-WAN network.

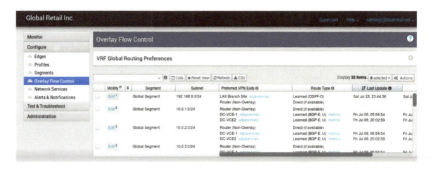

Figure 8.7 Global Routing View from VMware SD-WAN Orchestrator: Overlay Flow Control Table

Scaling Smarter with a Resource Aware Hub Cluster

For enterprises that need to scale, a hierarchical hub design with edge clusters can help them keep pace. This approach sets up sites where all branches from a region are consolidated into a regional hub site. This regional hub site includes a cluster of edges to accommodate increased capacity and throughput requirements placed on the hub site. The cluster will consist of multiple edges, each processing a portion of the network load, while providing additional redundancy.

Streamlining Mergers and Acquisitions

For enterprise organizations that are growing through mergers and acquisitions, VMware SD-WAN provides a simple mechanism to incorporate network assets of the acquired company.

A site that is not utilizing VMware SD-WAN could employ a one-way network address translation (NAT), providing the acquired company access to resources of its new parent company.

Since VMware SD-WAN also supports easy deployment of edge components, organizations could establish a network "beach head" where they could land new services and facilitate instance and application migration to the parent company's infrastructure.

Cost Reduction

VMware SD-WAN lets organizations take advantage of economical broadband links to support WAN connectivity, as well as as-a-service offerings that help minimize up-front costs.

Enhancing Cost Control

With VMware SD-WAN, organizations can utilize multiple WAN connections in a simple, manageable way. It lets network teams leave the complexity of the underlying WAN to the VMware SD-WAN. With VMware SD-WAN, enterprises can virtually extend network capabilities over both MPLS and the Internet, ensuring a network design that is cost-effective, without compromising quality. This flexible platform lets them utilize inexpensive broadband circuits while retaining the same level of performance.

The Dynamic Multi-Path Optimization protocol plays a key role in ensuring optimal performance. This link monitoring protocol examines the entire path between VMware SD-WAN data plane. It monitors for packet loss, jitter, and latency. Most link monitors consider only a limited range, and the state of a connection. Dynamic Multi-Path Optimization can utilize a variety of connections by applying per-packet load balancing. It selects the best connection for the type of packet that it is currently processing, whether transactional data or latency-sensitive voice or video.

Dynamic Multi-Path Optimization offers sub-second blackout and brownout protection. A link that is completely down is referred to as having a blackout condition. A link that is unable to deliver SLA for a given application is referred to as having a brownout condition.

Dynamic Multi-Path Optimization puts all the WAN circuits in active-active mode. In situations where it may not be possible to steer the traffic flow onto the better link, such as a single link deployment, or multiple links having issues at the same time, Dynamic Multi-Path Optimization can enable error correction for the duration of the disruption. It also enables application-aware dynamic per-packet steering, on-demand remediation, and overlay QoS.

With Dynamic Multi-Path Optimization, organizations can ensure optimal SD-WAN performance for the most demanding applications over any transport (Internet or hybrid); and any destination (on-premises or cloud). The result is assured application performance over any type of link.

In Focus: Business Services Firm Extends Cloud Services to Hundreds of Locations

A global provider of business services depends on its network infrastructure to connect more than 35,000 employees at 500 remote locations worldwide. The organization relies on cloud services to connect workers and offices across 65 countries.

As the organization grew, its legacy infrastructure began to show its age. It could no longer offer the bandwidth and performance required to support its essential cloud services. As complexity grew, network teams lacked the ability to handle corporate-wide network implementation and control.

To address the issue, the firm implemented an VMware SD-WAN by VeloCloud solution. This software-based solution enabled the firm to:

- Dramatically reduce CapEx and OpEx by replacing its legacy routers with more cost-effective edge devices.

- Deliver centralized visibility and management of the entire network, enabling the firm to easily add or modify network services whenever and wherever they are required.

- Enjoy improved network efficiency, for better performance on its cloud-based applications and higher sales.

In Focus: Fortune 500 Mining Company Gains an Edge with Big Data

A hundred-year-old mining company depends on its network to support more than 70 locations worldwide, and 50,000 employees. Microsoft Azure cloud services play an integral role at the organization, providing support for applications like geological mining and other analytics.

To transmit terabyte-sized files, the firm requires large amounts of bandwidth. However, the bandwidth on its existing infrastructure was not optimized to support rich media files, slowing processes and delaying production. IT managers also lacked efficient access to the Microsoft Azure cloud system, making it difficult to control and manage cloud services.

To gain control over its key cloud applications, the firm deployed an VMware SD-WAN solution. This software-based solution enabled the mining organization to:

- Transmit terabyte-sized files, while supporting unified communications.

- Boost bandwidth two to four times.

- Reduce deployment time from months to days.

- Gain centralized network visibility, control, and management.

- Take advantage of comprehensive, extensive data on geological landscape and mineral composition.

Before and After: The SD-WAN Difference

Before deploying SD-WAN, many enterprises backhauled all Internet and SaaS traffic to the datacenter firewall (Figure 8.8). Security Internet Gateway (SIG) is being used by branch sites with Internet-only connections to access MPLS resources. Element management is used for individual network devices configuration and monitoring.

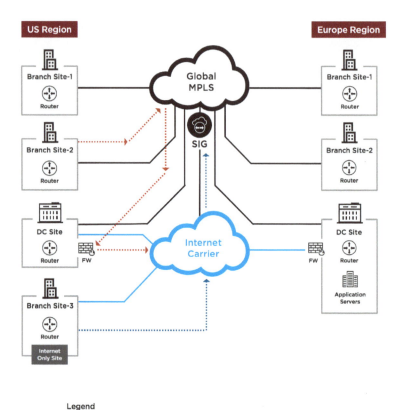

Figure 8.8 Enterprise Without SD-WAN

What has changed with SD-WAN? The VMware SD-WAN Orchestrator provides all the management, configuration, monitoring and troubleshooting and replaces the complexity when compared to element management (Figure 8.9).

The enterprise can utilize the regional and localized Internet links it prefers. Applications can be accessed in the cloud and on-premises using VMware SD-WAN devices, and take advantage of dramatic performance benefits in both environments.

VMware SD-WAN also enables site-to-site VPN (i.e. intrasite connectivity between U.S. regions) without using global MPLS circuits.

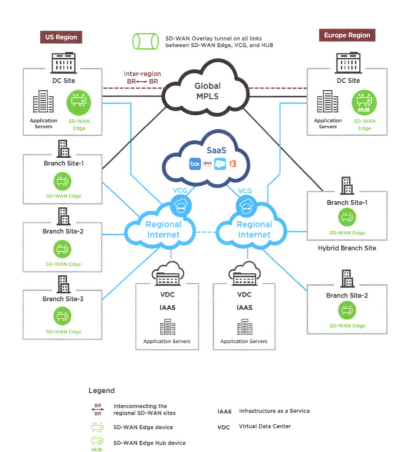

Figure 8.9 Enterprise With VMware SD-WAN

What You Need to Know

- Enterprises must deliver access to applications anywhere, from any environment, whether cloud or on-premises, while scaling and securing their environments.

- Enterprises are seeking better insight and control over their strategic management and unsanctioned applications.

- VMware SD-WAN delivers richer, deeper analytics that enable enterprises to take control of unsanctioned applications and gain insight for capacity planning.

- Utilizing a business policy-based approach lets enterprises enable prioritization at the business level and enjoy one-click provisioning of virtual services in the branch, the cloud, or the data center.

- VMware SD-WAN is an ideal platform to power business agility through DevOps by rapidly putting needed resources and specialized features in place.

Chapter 9

Conclusion

We hope this book has provided an informative overview of the basic concepts of SD-WAN, and how it enables organizations like yours to address their most significant challenges.

As network teams take on a more strategic role, their responsibilities have evolved beyond simply keeping the lights on. To keep pace in an increasingly complex, multi-cloud world, network teams need an infrastructure that is primed to spark innovation, enable superior experiences for customers, and enhance business agility.

VMware SD-WAN by VeloCloud delivers the foundation that organizations need to move forward in an increasingly dynamic environment. Whether you are connecting a small enterprise environment or a multinational corporation, VMware SD-WAN empowers you to enjoy greater control, more connectivity options, and assured performance across every branch site.

To learn more about how VMware SD-WAN by VeloCloud can benefit your organization, visit: http://www.velocloud.com/

Commonly Used Acronyms

AoC: Attestation of Compliance (retail)

CASB: Cloud access security broker

BYOD: Bring your own device

EHR: Electronic Health Record

EMR: Electronic Medical record

MPLS: Multiprotocol Label Switching

IaaS: Infrastructure-as-a-Service

IoT: Internet of Things

ISP: Internet Service Provider

OTT: Over-the-top architecture

PCI: Payment Card Industry (retail)

PCI-DSS: Payment Card Industry Data Security Standard

SaaS: Software-as-a-Service

SDN: Software-defined networking

SD-WAN: Software-defined WAN

uCPE: Universal customer premises equipment

VDI: Virtual Desktop Infrastructure

VNF: Virtual Network Function

VoIP: Voice over IP

WAN: Wide Area Network

References

1 "Cloud Computing Trends: 2018 State of the Cloud Survey," Rightscale

2 Interop ITX Research, August 2017

3 VNI Index, 2018

4 https://www.telecomramblings.com/2017/09/focus-makes-difference-sd-wan-vendors

5 "Stage 7" https://www.himssanalytics.org/emram

6 LoginVSI https://info.loginvsi.com/acton/attachment/25205/f-0121/1/-/-/-/-/State%20of%20the%20VDI%20and%20SBC%20Survey%202017%20Edition%20v2.1.pdf?sid=TV2:g4MGwTIJe

7 https://www.cdc.gov/nchs/fastats/electronic-medical-records.htm

8 https://www.vmware.com/content/dam/digitalmarketing/vmware/en/pdf/products/vmw-positive-impact-sd-wan-healthcare-esg-whitepaper.pdf

9 "Telemedicine to reach $40B by 2021" https://www.reuters.com/brandfeatures/venture-capital/article?id=29410

10 "Top Five Digital Transformation Trends in Retail," Daniel Newman, Forbes, March 2017.

11 "Top Five Digital Transformation Trends in Retail," Daniel Newman, Forbes, March 2017.

12 "Three Emerging Technologies Impacting the Construction Industry", February, 2018, Forbes

13 "IoT Trend Watch 2017," IHS Markit

14 "IoT Platforms: Enabling the Internet of Things," HIS Markit, 2016.

15 http://www.nam.org/Newsroom/Top-20-Facts-About-Manufacturing/

16 "What Everyone Must Know About Industry 4.0," Bernard Marr, Forbes, June 20, 2016

17 SD-WAN Enabling Digital Transformation in Manufacturing, IDC infographic sponsored by Comcast, March, 2018

18 SD-WAN Enabling Digital Transformation in Manufacturing, IDC infographic sponsored by Comcast, March, 2018

19 https://www.gartner.com/smarterwithgartner/4-trends-that-impact-how-midsize-enterprises-deal-with-it-vendors/

20 "IDC CloudView," IDC, April, 2017

Index

VMware SD-WAN Gateway
    Definition · 19
VMware SD-WAN Orchestrator
    Definition · 19
VMware SD-WAN Segmentation · 64

Z

Zero-touch provisioning · 76, 85, 86
Zigbee · 31

www.ingramcontent.com/pod-product-compliance
Lightning Source LLC
Chambersburg PA
CBHW041154050326
40690CB00004B/558